Hoover Institution Studies: 20

Socialism and Private Enterprise in Equatorial Asia

Socialism and Private Enterprise in Equatorial Asia: The Case of Malaysia and Indonesia

By

Roger A. Freeman

The Hoover Institution
on War, Revolution and Peace
Stanford University, Stanford, California
1968

Library of Congress Catalog Card Number: 67-31386

Printed in the United States of America

Preface

As we advance well into the second half of the United Nations' "Development Decade," disillusion about its promised world of plenty—and doubts about achieving such a world—are supplanting the earlier hope and enthusiasm. A few years ago it was expected that the gap between the major industrial powers and the less developed or backward countries would narrow substantially in the 1960's. The living standard, and the economic prospects, of the lower two-thirds of the world's population would rise in absolute as well as relative terms; increasingly, it was thought, wealth and prosperity would become more evenly spread.

This has not happened. To be sure, production and income are rising in most countries, but the rate of progress in many is far slower than that planned. Often such progress barely matches population growth and inflation, and in some areas production and income lag behind. In most areas except Europe, North America, and the older countries of the British Commonwealth, per-capita income and living standards are improving very slowly. In some spots they either are barely maintained or are declining. The United Nations Conference on Trade and Development (UNCTAD) reported in 1966 (*A Review of the Implementation of Recommendations of the Conference*), "Measured in terms of U.S. dollars converted at official exchange rates, the average *per-capita* income of the developed market economies increased by approximately $175 between 1960 and 1963, while that of the developing countries increased by about $8." [1]

[1] Whenever used, the sign $ means U.S. dollars; Malay dollars are shown as M $, Hongkong dollars as HK $.

The main theme and concern of the 44-nation conference on economic problems of the United Nations' Economic Commission for Asia and the Far East (ECAFE), which met in Tokyo in April 1967 for two weeks, was that "Progress in Asian economic development is 'distressingly slow' and the gap between the poor and rich countries is widening, not narrowing." Between 1958 and 1965 Gross Domestic Product per capita grew in the "developed countries" (North America, Europe, Oceania, Japan and South Africa) by 29%, in the "developing (i.e. all other) countries" by 16%.[2] The rich are getting richer, and though the poor are not generally getting poorer, the ratio between the rich and the poor is higher today than it was five or ten years ago, and there is no sign that the trend is changing.

Most Africans and Asians now subsist on a per-capita income below—or not much above—$100 a year, while income runs at about $1,000 to $1,500 in the major European nations and at almost $3,000 in the United States.

The prospect of a vast and widening contrast between the "have" and the "have-not" nations throws a dark cloud over hopes of sound and peaceful progress in the last third of the twentieth century, and threatens to lead to outbreaks of violence and war.

How can we explain these undesirable and, on the whole, unexpected trends? The first thought that comes to mind may well be this: the same basic forces that over the past century have expanded and enriched the economy of some countries, while keeping others poor, are still active and still push in the same direction. Meanwhile, postwar action for the rapid economic improvement of backward areas—such as establishment of political independence; technical and financial aid; expansion of education, health, and welfare programs; and

[2] *Statistical Yearbook, 1966*, United Nations, p. 29.

improvement in communications and public facilities—has been either inadequate, directed at the wrong objectives, or attempted by the wrong means. Could it be that none of the essential ingredients, the natural and human resources and their use, have changed sufficiently to reverse or modify a trend which has been in evidence for a long time?

The most obvious change in many Asian and African countries in the postwar period has been their advance from colonial to independent status and the substitution of government-to-government financial and technical aid for the earlier largely private investment by the European colonial powers. It was hoped that political independence and local economic planning and decision-making by their own nationals would be the key to a "take-off" to rapid development and prosperity for these countries. As it turned out, the key worked not very well, if at all.

Some of the less developed countries did make satisfactory progress, but they were the exceptions to the general rule. ECAFE reported in 1966 that per-capita food production in these areas was still below its prewar level, and many of the former net crop exporters were now using their scarce foreign exchange earnings, credits, or aid amounts, to import, not machinery, but basic foodstuffs from industrially leading countries. Aside from the question of necessity, this makes no economic sense whatsoever. Nor had mining, manufacturing, or trade made sufficient progress to compensate for the agricultural deficiencies.

There are many opinions on the cause for the disturbing and seemingly inalterable lag in many of the poorer countries, but there is no consensus. Scholars in the physical sciences, such as chemistry, physics, or biology, can usually discover cause-and-effect relationships by conducting large numbers of test series in which they isolate the various factors so as to identify the responsible one. Social scientists are not so fortunate. They cannot set up controlled experiments in which all factors but one are held constant. Entire countries or large numbers of human beings cannot be used as guinea pigs. Economists must consider a multiplicity of factors which simultaneously impinge on a country. We cannot as a rule, and at the present state of our knowledge, say with scientific certainty what force or economic policy caused one country to prosper and another to stagnate. But we can, by comparing results in a number of countries, arrive at some tentative conclusions on what makes an economy tick and what holds it back. Economics is far from from an exact science at this time, but analytical observation can yield at least a high degree of probability in regard to the favorable or unfavorable effect of specified economic methods or policies.

We must of course be very careful in making comparisons between countries which, inevitably, differ in more than one respect. We need to find countries which are as similar in their general environmental conditions as possible, but differ significantly in economic policy.

Two political-economic systems claim to offer the most direct and rapid avenues to prosperity: the free market or capitalist system, based on free enterprise, and the socialistic system of government ownership and direction of the means of production.

The advocates of free enterprise point to the experience and obvious success of the Western European countries and the United States as proof that theirs is the best and possibly even the only way to achieve high standards of living. The spokesmen for socialism reply that the capitalist countries rose through a painful process of ruthless mass exploitation that took a hundred to two hundred years. Socialists promise fulfillment within a few decades through a scientifically planned "command economy" which government directs and controls instead of letting the jungle of market competition rule. They point to the success of the Soviet Union, which, from a relatively backward stage, developed the world's second largest economy within less than 50 years.

But the experience of the Soviet Union has not been paralleled in less developed countries outside its realm. Studies by ECAFE show that during the postwar period the public sector in most Asian countries was growing both absolutely and relative to the total economy, that a multitude of ambitious development plans, generally tending toward a socialist pattern, led to "irrational allocation of investment, overemphasis on the development of infrastructure and heavy industry to the detriment of agriculture and export promotion, insufficient attention to the quality of human resources, and an inadequate rate of savings as main causes of the slow rate of growth in the decade of the fifties." Nor have these trends improved in the sixties. While world agricultural production now runs 10-12% per capita *above* its prewar level, it is about 5% *below* prewar in the ECAFE region, with Indonesia having the worst record. Traditional crop export countries have come to depend increasingly on food imports from industrial nations, and their inhabitants have less to eat than in the days when they were still under colonial rule.

There are few examples of two comparable nations with more or less similar natural conditions, one of which has followed free enterprise and the other the path of socialism. Among the approximately 120 countries on the face of the globe, probably no two offer as rich an opportunity to study the effect of diametrically opposed economic policies as do Malaysia and Indonesia. Located closely together, divided only by narrow straits, they share a benign growing climate; a profusion of largely identical natural resources; and a native population of Malay descent and language and of the Muslim faith. Both were colonies of European powers for many years and have gained their independence since World War II.

The contrast in their economic fortunes over the past 20 years is astounding: Malaysia boasts a remarkable record of growth and stability, while Indonesia's economy has steadily deteriorated and now lies in a shambles.

This may *suggest*, but does not necessarily *prove*, that socialism is responsible for Indonesia's woes and capitalism for Malaysia's prosperity. Some believe that it was not socialism that ruined Indonesia, but the incompetence of its government leaders. ("Socialism did not fail; it was never tried.") Others assert that Malaysia's success cannot be credited to its policy of giving free sway to capitalism, but to a unique and accidental combination of important resources with a sizeable, ambitious, and hard-working ethnic minority group.[3]

To learn more and faster than I could by continuing in the United States a study of the extensive literature about the postwar economic history of Malaysia and Indonesia and their present conditions and prospects, I visited the two countries in the summer and fall of 1966. My stay was too short for a thorough economic study. I hoped to—and did—"sniff the economic atmosphere." My findings and conclusions are outlined in this book. My general conclusion is this: the fact that capitalistic Malaysia has succeeded and socialistic Indonesia has failed, cannot be attributed simply to coincidence, accident, or luck. Policy played a major role. This does *not* necessarily mean that Indonesia would now be prospering had it

---

[3] Some observers feel that one reason for the difference in economic fortunes of postwar Indonesia and Malaysia is that the former won its independence by an armed struggle while the latter gained it by negotiation. Four years of internal warfare, from 1945 to 1949, were not only very costly to Indonesia, seriously delaying repair of war damages and restoration of the productive plant; they also intensified the hostile feelings of the Indonesians toward the Dutch and deprived Indonesia of potential aid. The Malays, however, permitted the British to return to their command posts at the end of the Japanese occupation, and to resume political control for another twelve years. Thus Malaysia reaped the benefit of peaceful development and continued British assistance, while Indonesia had to pay a high price for abruptly cutting its ties to the Netherlands.

adhered to capitalism or that Malaysia would be in misery had it chosen socialism, though this might well have been the outcome. Other factors, known and unknown, may have affected the results significantly and do bear part of the responsibility.

Only continued and more thorough studies in Malaysia and Indonesia and in many other countries, both prosperous and stagnant, can give us reliable answers to serve as guidelines for the policymakers of the nations that wish so desperately to lift themselves from their low status but have so far been making only slow progress. As of now, the case of Malaysia and Indonesia by itself does not conclusively prove the superiority of the free market system. But the comparison certainly suggests with a high degree of probability that at least in this case capitalism was more effective in creating sustained economic growth than socialism. It provides another important piece of evidence to support the proposition that "a direct relationship exists between the climate for individual enterprise and the rate of economic growth," as the Committee for Economic Development recently stated it.[4]

I want to express my appreciation to the many knowledgeable persons in Malaysia, Indonesia, Singapore, and in the United States who helped me gather information, patiently answered my questions, gave me valuable leads, and contributed material. I want to mention particularly Mr. John Lloyd III, First Secretary, U. S. Embassy in Kuala Lumpur; Mr. Siew Nim Chee, formerly Chief Economist of the National Bank of Malaysia, now financial adviser to Esso Standard Malaya, Ltd.; Mr. Harvey Stockwin, Malaysian correspondent of the *Far Eastern Economic Review;* Mr. J. A. Steenmejr, Manager of the Bank of America branch in Kuala Lumpur; and among Malaysian government officials especially Mr. Thong Yaw Hong, Director of the Economic Planning Unit in the

[4] *How Low Income Countries Can Advance Their Own Growth,* Committee for Economic Development, 1966, p. 23.

Prime Minister's Department, and Mr. Abu Kassim, Director of the National Production Authority. I was greatly helped by Mr. Roger Sullivan, First Secretary, U. S. Embassy in Singapore, and Mr. Gordon Donald, Jr., First Secretary, U. S. Embassy in Djakarta, and by extensive information and documentation supplied by Professor Mohammad Sadli of the University of Indonesia.

My sincere thanks go to the gentlemen who were kind enough to review the manuscript and give me the benefit of their criticism, advice, and suggestions: His Excellency Tan Sri Ong Yoke Lin, Malaysian Ambassador to the United States; Professor Warren S. Hunsberger of The American University (then a Ford Foundation representative in Kuala Lumpur); Professor Hamlin Robinson of the Graduate School of Public and International Affairs, University of Pittsburgh (then with the Stanford Research Institute); Mr. R. H. Hopper, Vice President of American Overseas Petroleum Limited in New York; Mr. Jan Muelder, Financial Manager of Caltex Pacific Indonesia and American Overseas Petroleum Limited in Djakarta; and Dr. Clifton R. Wharton, Jr. of the Agricultural Development Council in New York. It was a pleasure exchanging notes with Dr. Willy Linder, editor of the *Neue Zuercher Zeitung*, while we both were busily gathering data in Djakarta as well as after our return.

They all helped greatly, but of course the responsibility for the facts I present and for the opinions I express is exclusively my own.

If this book succeeds in arousing interest in the comparative economics of Malaysia and Indonesia and leads to further and more thorough studies of the role which economic policy plays in shaping the fortune of developed and undeveloped countries, it will have served its purpose.

ROGER A. FREEMAN

STANFORD, CALIFORNIA
AUGUST 1967

Table of Contents

CHAPTER I

Postwar Economic Growth
In Equatorial Asia

In journeying through the lands of South Asia — or of Africa or Latin America — the traveler cannot but be struck by the drastic contrast between two types of countries: some are evidently prospering, showing signs of both stability and growth, steadily moving toward an ever brighter future. Others seem unable to lift themselves above misery and starvation; despite generous and continued doses of foreign aid, they appear to slide ever deeper into the morass of deprivation and hopelessness. The traveler will ask: why are some countries thriving in warm sunshine while others shiver under black clouds?

The chance presence of natural wealth, of valuable physical resources, offers itself as an easy explanation of why some are rich and others are poor. But this turns out to be too easy an explanation; closer study reveals that the correlation between measurable material resources and economic growth is not as high as we might think. Of course, a country may be affluent just because it sits on top of an oil pool. But very few do. Moreover, the oil had been there for aeons, but the country's residents lived in abject poverty until a decade or two ago, when foreign technicians and capital explored the substrata and turned them into a source of wealth. It was that action of foreign engineers and entrepreneurs that converted destitution to opulence. Observers who credit the spectacular development of the United States in the past 200 years to its natural resources might profitably ponder why the American continent's former residents were barely able to feed themselves during the 10,000 or so years of their occupancy, while the new settlers required but a tiny fraction of that time — about one or two percent — to make the land and themselves the richest on earth.

One of the most significant facts of economic life, though often forgotten, is that some of the most prosperous countries on earth are among the poorest in resources. Switzerland, for example, possesses none of the basic materials essential to modern industrial growth, but it has long enjoyed greater financial well-being, political stability, and freedom from war and internal disorder than any other country. Scandinavia offers parallels. Japan, which lacks most of the natural resources to feed its basic industries and has to import much of the needed raw material, has experienced the fastest economic growth rate of any country over the past 15 years— and probably over the past 100 years. In contrast, India, from which Japan imports some of those vital raw materials, seems unable to rise above the starvation level.

A substantial share of the minerals and other natural products without which the advanced countries could not operate their industrial apparatus or maintain their high living standards comes from countries on the verge of destitution. Are the supplier countries destitute because of exploitation by their colonial masters or former masters, as the "conventional wisdom" has long been telling us? Are colonialism or neocolonialism and capitalist imperialism ("necolim") responsible for the fact that the supplier countries are poor while the user countries are rich?

If colonial exploitation is the secret of capital accumulation and the source of riches for the major European powers, how do we explain the growth of the world's wealthiest country, the United States, which never owned colonies? If colonialism means exploitation, why did the Dutch East Indies, soon after gaining independence in 1949, begin a rapid downward slide, while the Netherlands, bereft of a precious possession with nearly ten times its own population, prospered more than ever before? The story of the imperialist colonial masters waxing rich at the expense of captive and oppressed natives who are being deprived of their country's natural wealth — and the fruits of their labor — was told by Lenin, and has often been repeated because it serves as a superb alibi for failure and obviates the necessity of facing unpleasant facts as they are, it still is widely taken at face value. But much of it is a myth, as appears from the findings of the "Colonialism in Africa" research project, now nearing completion, headed by Dr. Peter Duignan, Director of African Studies at the Hoover Institution.[1] The possession of colonies may often have resulted in a net drain rather than been a source of wealth to the European "mother country."[2]

When the colonial era ended within a few years after World War II, a long period began during which Europe's economies flourished, and many or most of the newly independent countries suffered increasing disappointment in the progress and rate of growth they were able to achieve even with massive assistance. Many of them found their economic and financial troubles multiplying. When so many of the countries which used to be called backward or underdeveloped failed to show the rate of advance they had expected, a semantic remedy was sought by labeling them "developing countries," though it seems amply clear that the one thing they have in common and which makes them a problem is that they are

[1] Lewis Gann and Peter Duignan, *Burden of Empire,* New York, Praeger, 1967.
[2] Other recent studies with similar findings: D. K. Fieldhouse, *The Colonial Empires,* Weidenfeld and Nicolson, London, 1966; Ian Brook, *The One-Eyed Man Is King,* Putnam, New York, 1966.

NOT developing, at least not at a rate sufficient to bring them closer to the level of the industrial nations.

The obvious reluctance and even resistance which investors and entrepreneurs from the major capitalist countries show about becoming heavily involved in the "developing countries" offer an ironic comment on the popular thesis of "neocolonialist exploitation." [3] Even tax and other incentives offered by the U. S. Government, for instance, have done little to induce American corporations and individuals to commit themselves more deeply in less developed—and supposedly exploitable—countries. They seem to prefer expanding their operations in industrialized lands where competition is keen and U. S. tax penalties are high. Nor has the existence of rich mineral deposits or the potential of high crop yields proven sufficiently attractive to offset the political-economic conditions which some of the less developed countries impose or threaten to impose on foreign investors and operators.

If the presence of natural resouces is not the final, or even a major, determinant of a country's economic fortunes, then such a determinant must be its human resources—unless we assume that there is no possibility of a rational explanation, that poverty and wealth are allocated among nations fortuitously and haphazardly as, according to some, they are among individuals.

That human resources are a major factor governing a country's rate of progress, few will question. It appears quite likely that the caliber of human resources is the *controlling* factor,

[3] The former financial and industrial editor of *The Times* (London), W. M. Clarke, described in *Private Enterprise in Developing Countries* (Oxford, Pergamon Press, 1966) the decline of private investment in nonindustrial countries and the major reasons behind this trend: "What lies behind much of the thinking of the developing countries is the idea that there somehow is something wrong with the pursuit of profit by commercial concerns among the poor and needy." (p. 8.) Though many of those countries do not deliberately *intend* to discourage foreign investment, their policies could not be much different if they did.

and not a few observers would equate "caliber" with formal education. Too many of the colonial regimes either had not sufficiently promoted adequate schooling for the indigenous population or had plainly neglected it, even at the primary level. Political independence opened the doors to bright opportunities in education.

Students of development tend to view formal education as the true key to progress and have expressed their faith in it strongly and repeatedly.[4] Governments of the new countries were more than eager to accept their advice, and set about to multiply educational offerings for their young citizens. In this endeavor most were successful. Rapid expansion of school systems is probably the proudest record and the most remarkable tangible achievement of many of the new countries. Illiteracy rates were sharply cut in the less developed regions and literacy there expanded more in the past twenty years than in all prior history. In Indonesia, for example, the literacy rate grew from 6% of the indigenous population at the end of the colonial regime to 43% in the early 1960's.

But economic returns on the huge investments in education have so far fallen far short of hopes and promises, as the disappointing record of economic growth seems to indicate. While of course universal and improved education is an eminently desirable goal in itself that justifiably rates top priority in available resources almost everywhere, it appears that expectations of direct and prompt returns must be scaled down.

There are, in fact, many examples of poor countries in which educated but underemployed and discontented groups pose a problem and a real threat—or where governmental

[4] *Policy Conference on Economic Development and Investment in Education*, Paris, OECD, 1962.

Education and Economic Development, ed. C. Arnold Anderson and Mary Jean Bowman, Chicago, Aldine Publishing Co., 1965.

Education and the Development of Nations, ed. John W. Hanson and Colin S. Brembeck, New York, Holt, Rinehart & Winston, 1966.

payrolls are deliberately overloaded in an attempt to render a discontented intellectual proletariat less dangerous. It seems that often education *follows rather than precedes* economic development. In other words, when a country become affluent it can afford to and commonly does devote a greater proportion of its resources to education. Indeed, it may well be that the same or similar human traits make for both economic advancement and the pursuit of education. But the postwar record casts doubt on the proposition that a backward country can achieve rapid economic growth just by multiplying its educational offerings. Far more may be involved than just the building and staffing of new schools.

By "human resources" we mean not merely sheer numbers; if we meant only that, India and mainland China would be at the top of the economic ladder, and not near its bottom (where they are). The term refers to quality, and it indicates certain characteristics—intelligence, drive, self-discipline, responsibility, and similar traits—which together assure greater economic competence: a greater capacity to master man's environment and bend it to his needs and wants.

Until not so many years ago it was generally taken for granted that anthropological factors were the prime determinants of the rate of a nation's progress and attainable goals. Certain ethnic groups manifested great prowess in pursuing economic objectives and achieved remarkable heights of success which could not be explained by purely environmental factors. Even today we see in many countries, living under the same general conditions, some ethnic groups rising to the top and remaining there while others form the lower strata of society. Chinese minorities throughout Southeast Asia, Indians in East Africa from Uganda to Durban and in Fiji, Armenians in the Near East, and Jews in many countries demonstrate a greater economic effectiveness than the indigenous majority. Certain other ethnic groups are typically less successful in the competition for material goods and fill the ranks of the poor, from which only a few manage to rise.

Though the assumption of an anthropological or genetic cause for these differences has lost much or most of its support in recent decades and is now held to be without foundation by many scholars in the field, it still exerts a distinct influence on public policies, if sometimes unconsciously and seldom admittedly.

In the nineteenth century the colonial powers were certain that "natives," whether educated or not, were generally unable to compete with Europeans, and that they required special protection. The theory of a dualistic colonial economic policy was developed by the Dutch economist J. H. Boeke, based largely on experiences in the Dutch East Indies. It has long been discarded and is now in academic ill repute. But many or most countries with multi-ethnic populations at differing economic levels even today pursue dualistic economic policies. They aim to protect, assist, advance or prefer members of less successful groups, to ease their way into economic life, to reduce the competition to which they are subjected, and to lower the bars or render greater aid to them. A few countries place restrictions, by law or custom, on ethnic minorities deemed to be inferior in certain characteristics. Conversely, ethnic minorities which tend to be economically more successful often are handicapped by obstacles, whether formalized by statute or observed by common practice or "gentleman's agreement," so as to prevent them from dominating the economy or exerting disproportionate power or influence. A quota system (such as *numerus clausus*) is often applied to supersede in fact (though not necessarily in name) the official principle of equal opportunity.

It is unfortunate that in this area emotionalism and prejudice seem to have become so potent and pervasive that rational, dispassionate discussion seems all but impossible.

Important as the question of the role of genetic factors in economic growth is, it is probably at the present time unanswerable. Attempts at developing answers more often become exchanges of invective than factual and scholarly presentations. Consequently, it must for the time being remain moot whether certain intrinsic differences in human characteristics among various national groups influence or determine their economic progress.

The debate over the roots of economic growth has for some years focused largely on the role of economic policies. This is so partly because the type of policy pursued could well be the most powerful influence, and partly because policy is a matter of choice and manipulation. It is more directly subject to governmental action than most of the other factors and therefore needs to be studied more thoroughly so that it can be formed intelligently. In the immediate postwar period, the majority of "development economists" left no doubt that they regarded stronger government intervention to be the surest way to economic bliss. Comprehensive governmental plans were formed to establish and expand certain industries, and to set or guide investment, prices, wages, profits, and most of the other factors which in a free economic system are commonly left to the play of market forces. It is not surprising that particularly the newly independent countries, anxious to "catch up," tended to follow this path of central planning and control—often coupled with government ownership—more or less along socialistic lines. Only a few of them pursued a strictly private-enterprise policy.

To be sure, governments of many industrial countries also developed economic plans, but of a different type. They were more in the nature of projections or long-range forecasts of what the economy was likely to do, so as to give the budget makers guidelines for planning personnel, finances, and a necessary infrastructure—roads, health and education facilities, and other traditionally public programs and facilities. France, Holland, Sweden, Norway, Japan, and other countries prepared what has been called "indicative plans," shaped with the cooperation, or under the auspices, of private industry. Often they had only vague governmental sanction, if any, and all lacked the mandatory features typical of comprehensive or socialistic multi-year plans.

Rapid advance in those countries that did little or no central planning, and the failure of most of the comprehensive central plans, has caused development economists to have second thoughts. They seem to be less certain today than they once were that centralized planning and increased governmental action are the best answer to development problems in backward countries.

In Asia, it seemed that of two neighboring countries the one that relied on private enterprise almost always did better than the centrally planned country. This is certainly true in the case of Thailand and Burma, and in the case of Japan, the Republic of China (Taiwan), and Hongkong on one side, and India, Pakistan and mainland (Red) China on the other. "China's gross national product is thought to be one-fifth smaller today than it was when the Great Leap Forward came to grief. In neighboring Japan a hundred million people produce a national income as large as that of China, which has a population six to seven times as numerous." [5] The troubles of India and Pakistan are well known.

But the most telling case is that of Indonesia and Malaysia. Malaysia has consistently followed a private enterprise policy; its government has tried to improve the political-economic atmosphere for industrial and commercial investment and expansion but has not commanded it or even participated in it. The first two Malay plans (1956-60 and 1961-65) and the

[5] Werner Klatt, "China's New Leap Forward," *Far Eastern Economic Review*, July 21, 1966.

present First Malaysia Plan (1966-70) are of the indicative type used in western European countries.

Indonesia's government, upon gaining independence in 1949, left no doubt that it aimed at creating a socialist state. It let privately held corporations, which conducted virtually all of the country's large-scale economic activities, operate for a few more years, but announced that it would nationalize the major industries. It so did between 1958 and 1963. After taking over all Dutch businesses in 1958-60 and placing many others under close supervision, Indonesia adopted a comprehensive eight-year plan in 1960 which was so ambitious it could not be carried out. It soon broke down.

How do the economic fortunes of Malaysia and Indonesia in the postwar period compare? The following data were taken from the two most recent issues of the *Economic Survey of Asia and the Far East* (for 1965 and 1966) by ECAFE.[6]

Malaysia's per-capita income at over $300 (the most recent estimate for 1966 is M$ 963 = US$ 321) is second only to Japan among Asiatic nations and five to six times that of Indonesia, which has the *lowest* per-capita income shown. This is the more remarkable because Indonesia has a more fertile (volcanic) soil; certain major resources, such as oil, which Malaysia lacks; a far larger market (about ten times the population); and a lower rate of population growth—2.2%—than Malaysia's 3.1%, which is among the highest in the world. Moreover, Indonesia received about $3 billion in foreign aid during the postwar period and Malaysia almost none.

According to the cited ECAFE report for 1966 (p. 100), gross domestic product (in constant prices) grew between 1955 and 1965 at an annual average of 6.9% in Malaysia, an average of 1.7% in Indonesia. This means, on a *per-capita* basis, an annual growth of 2.0% in Malaysia, an average an-

[6] Economic Commission for Asia and the Far East, United Nations, Bangkok, 1966 and 1967, respectively.

nual *decline* of 0.4% in Indonesia. The Malaysian rate is not impressive compared with Thailand's 3.0%, Taiwan's 4.1%, or Japan's spectacular 8.5%, but it ranks above the average for "developing" countries in the East Asian region.

In most less developed countries, agriculture is by far the biggest sector of the economy. Its general importance to economic development is apparent from the well-known fact that even Western countries financed most of their early industrial growth (industrial revolution) from argricultural surpluses.

In its cited report for 1965 ECAFE reported (p. 163), "During the postwar period, from 1952-53 to 1964-65, the countries with the highest rate of growth in agricultural production were China (Taiwan) and Thailand, both with an average rate of 4.6 percent, significantly exceeding the rate of population growth. The country with the lowest growth rate was Indonesia at 1.0 percent, which was far below the population growth rate of 2.2 percent. . . . In the States of Malaya, the rate of agricultural growth was also significantly higher than the population growth rate. The difference between the two rates is small in other countries."

The same report shows (p. 273) that on a *per-capita* basis food production in Malaysia improved 40% between 1952-53 and 1964-65 but slightly declined in Indonesia.[7] This seems to confirm the impression of several observers that the Indonesian people had less to eat after 16 years of independence than they had in colonial days. Meanwhile the country used up much of its accumulated capital, and a large part of its productive plant became inoperative.

Malaysia and Indonesia are among the world's leading producers of tin and natural rubber. The output of tin concen-

[7] The 1966 ECAFE report shows (p. 233) an 18% increase in food production in Indonesia from 1964 to 1965, compared with a 14% cumulative increase over the preceding 11-year period, that is from 1953 to 1964. This contrasts with general observations of the country's food situation and the figure should not be accepted at face value until subsequently confirmed.

trates jumped 66% in Malaysia between 1958 and 1965, and *fell* 37% in Indonesia. Simultaneously, rubber output expanded 21% in Malaysia, in Indonesia only 2%. Palm oil production increased 110% in Malaysia between 1958 and 1965, in Indonesia only 13%. In the production of rice, the area's most important staple food, the discrepancy was not as great: output grew 30% in Indonesia, 48% in Malaysia during the mentioned period.[8]

Malaysia's exports increased 38% between 1958 and 1964; Indonesia's shrank 13%.[9] Malaysia's foreign currency reserve substantially increased, while Indonesia's dwindled to almost nothing—until the country was unable to meet its overdue foreign debt commitments or pay for even the most essential imports. It had to go hat in hand to its creditors and even to its former colonial master to beg for deferrals and new credits.

The value of the Malay dollar remained perfectly stable (3 to the U. S. dollar) throughout the postwar period. The cost of living rose only 3% between 1959 and 1966, while Indonesian prices multiplied more than 2,000 times between 1958 and 1966, largely because of the government's constant and excessive use of the banknote printing press.

The number of examples could be multiplied. But the picture is clear enough from the figures given above: in the years since gaining independence, Malaysia, without foreign aid [10] —except for military assistance against a Chinese-sponsored communist uprising and aggression from Indonesia ("confrontation"),—experienced high prosperity, while Indonesia, potentially one of the world's richest countries, deteriorated rapidly into bankruptcy. Indonesia's industrial production is now running at an average of only 25% of plant capacity.[11]

---

[8] *Statistical Yearbook, 1966,* United Nations, pp. 136, 139, 149, 197.

[9] *Ibid.,* p. 397.

[10] Not counting a small DLF (Development Loan Fund) loan and IBRD (World Bank) credits.

[11] ECAFE report, 1966, p. 102.

Was Malaysia's rise due to sheer luck, or was it the result of its economic policies? Was Indonesia's fall caused by its socialistic experiments or just by unfortunate circumstances? A 1961 ECAFE survey blamed Indonesia's decline on a failure of management by government. Does this mean only the incompetence of the Sukarno government, which did not achieve (or even approach) its goals, or were the goals and methods wrong? Could any other government trying to nationalize Indonesia's businesses according to socialist lines have been successful in propelling its economy upward? Or are bungling and mismanagement inevitable when government takes over a privately managed economy? Was the inability of the Sukarno government to manage the industrial and commercial enterprises and plantations efficiently a characteristic not of the persons then in power but of any government that attempts to do likewise? What lessons can other countries in similar circumstances draw from the Indonesian-Malaysian example?

Could it be that Malaysia succeeded because more than a third of its population is of Chinese descent and seemingly more effective in a free economy, whether by sheer hard work or by special talent, while Indonesia's residents include only 3% Chinese—not enough to provide the needed energy? If so, what was the contribution of the Europeans—mostly British in Malaysia, mostly Dutch in Indonesia—who never accounted for more than a fraction of 1% of the population? Was it the continued working of Europeans in Malaysia, as against the expulsion of the Dutch from Indonesia in 1958 that made the then mild contrast so dramatic in the ensuing years?

The short time I spent in the two countries does not enable me to provide firm answers to most of these questions, let alone to document opinions I formed. But I shall try in the next two chapters to provide some more facts from which the reader may draw his conclusions.

CHAPTER II
Malaysia's Free Enterprise Economy

Absence of the type of currency restrictions imposed by most other Asiatic countries impresses on the foreign visitor to Malaysia at the outset that he is entering a free country. He may exchange his U. S. dollars or British pounds for Malay dollars anywhere he wishes and at any rate offered. He can reconvert them whenever he pleases, at about the same rate less a customary bank margin. He is not limited in the amount of money he may bring in or take out, he need not report how much money he carries, and he will look in vain for a black market in currency. Nobody will accost him about exchanging dollars. Nor can he buy Malay banknotes at a rate lower than posted, official, or market rates in Hongkong, Singapore, or New York—as he can when he needs Indian, Pakistani, Vietnamese, Burmese, Cambodian or many other types of currency. The Malay dollar can be freely traded—and has been absolutely steady at three to the U. S. dollar (one Malay dollar = 33 U. S. cents) throughout the postwar period—in contrast to many other currencies which have been losing value. Prices have remained perfectly stable. All of this suggests that the Malaysian government has been keeping its budget in a reasonable balance and has not been resorting to the printing press to finance ambitious development plans or devise glittering schemes at the end of a rainbow. Despite such failure to pursue a fiscal policy which many contemporary economists deem essential to rapid development, the country has grown faster economically than most others.

The U. S. Army's *Handbook for Malaysia and Singapore* (July 1965, GPO), an excellent compilation of facts, commented that in Malaysia, "Ideological concepts have not played a very noticeable part in shaping economic policy. The main objective in 1965 was economic growth, and the government recognized that the surest and speediest way to obtain it was to encourage private enterprise. The government's role was conceived to be primarily to create an environment in which private enterprise could function most effectively. . . ."

While this is a correct description of the Malaysian government's economic policy, it goes too far in attributing it to pragmatic aims only. The Malaysian government is, of course, eager to promote economic growth, as is every other government in the region and in the world, yet many governments pursue a course of steadily increasing government direction, control, or ownership of the means of production and of other major economic activities.

In Malaysia, I found a general belief in official and business circles that the country's improvement and prosperity were related to the liberal economic policies it had been following.

My hosts emphasized that Malaysia, in contrast to most of its neighbors—and in fact to most nations—has received very little foreign financial aid, and almost none from the United States. Nor has its government attempted or undertaken huge publicly financed development schemes in the industrial or commercial sphere, except for opening suitable land to private developers and building essential public facilities (infrastructure). Yet it has done better than many of those other countries in attracting private investment—from local residents as well as from abroad—and has consistently shown sound economic growth rates with an average annual increase in the gross domestic product of 6.4% between 1960 and 1965 —the highest reported rate in Asia, save for Japan and the Republic of China (Taiwan). Its citizens now enjoy Asia's second highest per-capita income, exceeded only by Japan, and not counting the two city enclaves of Hongkong and Singapore, which have no agricultural, low-income hinterland.

These are remarkable accomplishments. But I could not help gaining the impression from talks with governmental and civic leaders in Malaysia that they *are* ideologically committed, that they believe in free enterprise not only because it promotes economic growth but because it is part of their philosophy, their conviction of what government ought to do or should not do. That belief seems to be firmly grounded in the long tradition and history of Malaysia, which gained its political independence only ten years ago.

The peninsula of Malaya was long divided into a number of independent sultanates which came more or less under direct British control in the course of the nineteenth century. British settlement gained firm footing with the acquisition in 1819 by Sir Thomas Stamford Raffles of a desolate tiny island at the peninsula's southernmost point. Being strategically located on the narrow Straits of Malacca, across the shipping lane to China and the Pacific, it grew into the area's queen city, Singapore.

While the Malay states continued under local rulers, governmental powers were actually exercised by British "residents" whose "advice" the sultan was forced to accept on all matters save the Muslim religion. In World War II Malaya suffered severely under the Japanese occupation from 1942 to 1945: plantations, mines, roads, railways, and bridges were heavily damaged. Much equipment was removed or left to deteriorate, estates were left untended, and labor was used for war purposes.

But postwar rehabilitation was rapid, damage and facilities were restored within a few years. Then "the emergency" started. An armed communist revolt, directed from mainland

China and 99% manned by Chinese, began in 1948 and soon
assumed threatening proportions. When the guerrillas assassi-
nated British High Commissioner Sir Henry Gurney in 1951,
a professional soldier, Sir Gerald Templer, was put in charge
of operations. With ruthless determination Sir Gerald broke
the back of the communist guerrilla force within two years,
although it took another six years, until 1960, to wipe out the
last remnants of the resistance. Ever since, a strong anticommunist spirit has pervaded Malaysia. To commemorate the
victory over the communist rebellion, and as a tribute to those
who won it, a grateful country erected near the Parliament
buildings a magnificent monument which is visited by all who
come to Kuala Lumpur.

Malaya gained its independence from Great Britain in 1957
by peaceful means. It is a constitutional monarchy, with individual states under local sultans who elect one among themselves as king for a five-year term. The government in fact is
chosen by a popularly elected parliament and has remained in
the same hands since before independence. The Alliance
Party, a coalition of Malay, Chinese, and Indian groups with
conservative leanings, has remained in firm control, and won
125 out of 159 seats in the Federal Parliament at the 1964 elections. Prime Minister Tunku (Prince) Abdul Rahman has
been the leader of the government for the past dozen years.
Direction of economic affairs has been in the hands of Deputy
Prime Minister Tun Abdul Razak, an unusually capable and
dynamic man who is entitled to much of the credit for Malaysia's outstanding record of achievement. It is typical of the
man that under his orders in the "control rooms" which are
maintained in all state and district centers, emphasis in charts
and reports is placed not on accomplishments but on short-
falls, so that these will be followed up and corrected without
delay.

Singapore, with three-fourths of its population of Chinese

descent, remained a self-governing Crown colony until 1963, when demands for full independence became overwhelming. But there was much doubt whether the city could form a country of its own. To merge it with Malaya would have resulted in a country with a Chinese majority, a prospect which the Malays did not relish. A solution was then found by adding parts of Northern Borneo—Sabah and Sarawak—to form with Malaya and Singapore the new country of Malaysia in 1963. But this still left about as many Chinese as Malays, and with the Chinese typically showing greater drive and economic advance and pushing hard under dynamic political leadership, the Malays became increasingly unhappy with the union and finally sought a divorce. In September 1965 Singapore became an independent republic which, to the surprise of many observers, is doing exceedingly well though it comprises only a small island of 224 square miles with fewer than 2 million inhabitants.

The formation of Malaysia in 1963 was sharply protested by Indonesia's President Sukarno, who soon proceeded to military action, with several attempts at invasion. This "confrontation" as it was called, imposed hardships on Malaysia by cutting off most of its large Indonesian trade and by multiplying defense outlays. It also accelerated Indonesia's economic ruin.

Malaysia, which has long maintained only small armed forces, was able to fight off the "confrontation" with British and Australian help. Indonesian aggression ceased after the new government came to power in the fall of 1965.

Malaysia now consists of the Malay peninsula and the Sabah and Sarawak regions of Northern Borneo. With an area of 127,000 square miles, it is considerably smaller than California and has about half as large a population concentrated in the western part of the Malay peninsula. Lying entirely within a few degrees of the equator, the country has a tropical climate which changes little during the year and enjoys a perpetual growing season. Daily minimum temperatures average 72° (maximum is 91°) with a steady 75% to 85% humidity and ample rain from six to eight inches a month, with only modest seasonal variations.

Malaysia's birthrate of 39 per 1,000 is among the highest in the world. It is slightly down from the rate of 46 in 1956, but more than twice Japan's current rate of 17.7. The government would like to cut the birthrate in half—but this will not be easy to accomplish. But even when at its highest birthrate, Malaysia has been able to enlarge its food production and national income *on a per-capita basis.*

MAJOR NATURAL RESOURCES

Malaysia does not have the fertile volcanic soil of Indonesia, and it lacks almost completely the modern energy sources which form the basis for industrial growth elsewhere: it has no coal, no oil and no gas (except for a few small wells in Sarawak), no significant hydroelectric potential. It depends for fuel almost completely on imports, from its more favored neighbors and other sources. Agriculture still is the country's major industry: more than half the labor force is employed in farming, fishing, or forestry. At least three-fourths of the Malay peninsula is covered by tropical rain forests, nearly impenetrable jungle, swamps and mountains; less than one-fifth of the land area is under cultivation.

None of the major commercial crops—rubber, palm oil, coconut—are indigenous. Chinese and British planters introduced them over long periods of trial and error and then developed them for export purposes.

Rubber, by far the most important of Malaysia's products, is a native of Brazil, whence seeds were smuggled to London's Kew Gardens to be grown in hothouses for possible use in colonies with suitable soil and climate. In 1877 the first attempts were made to grow rubber on the Malay peninsula, and commercial plantings began in 1895. The simultaneous appearance of the automobile and the spectacular expansion of its use in the succeeding quarter century—and ever since—multiplied many times the demand for rubber and spurred its production. Malaysia is now the world's largest producer of natural rubber, accounting for about 40% of the total supply. Almost two-thirds of the peninsula's cultivated area is given over to rubber, which provides close to one-half of the country's export earnings and about one-third of the budgetary revenue, while keeping almost one-fourth of its work force busy. The country's leaders are not very happy over this heavy dependence on a single product with a fluctuating price and an uncertain future. However, until other crops and industries are sufficiently developed to take its place, rubber must and does receive prime attention.

Prior to World War II, natural rubber was unique and irreplaceable. It no longer is. The exigencies of the war, with most of the supplies of the major Western powers cut off, brought a forced development of synthetic rubber, with great improvements in quality and reduced production costs. A technical breakthrough made synthetic rubber competitive with natural rubber in the postwar period, and by 1962 it occupied a bigger share of the rubber market than the natural product. The United States now turns out 60% of the world's synthetic rubber. Particularly since the emergence of the so-called stereo-regular rubbers, the synthetic product has been gaining sharply on the natural product, and from all appearances will continue to do so. The Soviet Union is Malaysia's biggest rubber customer.

Malaysia, as the world's leading natural rubber producer, did not take the advance of synthetic rubber lying down. It fought back. While the local main complaint was, and still is, directed at the steady decline of rubber prices [1]—from 36 cents (U.S.) per pound in 1960 to 24 in 1965, 18 in the autumn of 1967 and still falling—the industry's leaders recognize that natural rubber must compete or go under. An intentional price-maintenance agreement or program—something that several "developing" countries desire or demand for their principal export products—would only lead to a more rapid replacement of the natural product by synthetics. A Malayan Study Commission (Mudie Commission) concluded in 1953: "Malaya can do nothing about the price of synthetic rubber; it can only conform to it." Malaya's Rubber Research Institute, established in 1923, multiplied its efforts to increase the efficiency of natural rubber production by a shift to higher-yield types, improved methods of tapping with ladders, soil preparation and other means of providing a better product at a lower price. Malaysia has been, and intends to continue to be, a producer of high-quality rubber which can command a premium price in the market.

Rubber trees generally produce latex from about the fifth or sixth to the thirty-fifth year, after which they rapidly decline. Regular replacement of over-age trees is therefore essential to the maintenance of output. It is the failure to replace old trees and poor management in general that have accounted for the sharp decline in the rubber production of Indonesia since the Dutch plantations were nationalized and their owners and managers expelled in 1958-60.

Malaya, however, has managed to increase steadily its rubber production and to match price declines with improved efficiency. Following the recommendations of the above-mentioned study commission, replanting grants, administered by the rubber industry and financed from imposts on rubber

[1] Each decline of one cent per pound reduces Malaysia's export earnings by almost $7 million.

exports, were established in 1955. The replanting program encourages growers to substitute new trees for over-age trees, and high-yield trees for those of lower yield. Grants of M$ 750 to M$ 800 per acre are being paid to smallholders, and lesser amounts to estates, for replanting. The program was so enthusiastically received that, by 1966, 82% of the estate acreage and 57% of the smallholders' acreage had been replanted with high-yield varieties. This has been one of the most ambitious and successful agricultural modernization programs anywhere.

The annual harvest on estates that used to average 300 to 400 pounds per acre a year on the original trees and had grown to 490 pounds by 1955, jumped to 719 pounds by 1960, and to 898 pounds by 1966. It may soon run close to 1,000 pounds average, and already exceeds 2,500 pounds on a few plantations.

Smallholders have always used more primitive methods, but even they have made substantial progress, with the average yield rising from 350 pounds per acre in 1953 to 450 pounds in 1963.

Smallholdings are defined as units of less than 100 acres, but four-fifths of them cover less than 25 acres, and most measure only 3 to 5 acres. They are mostly owned by Malay peasants, and also some Chinese and Indians, who subsist largely on rice, maize, sweet potatoes, livestock, and fish, but who eagerly seized the opportunity to grow a cash crop which produces the year around. Smallholders now account for more than one-half the country's rubber acreage and are being helped by the government in many ways: agricultural education and extension services, aid with drainage, irrigation, land development and settlement plans, credit and marketing arrangements, etc.

Most rubber estates (over 100 acres) are in the hands of non-Malays, with the smaller and middle-sized plantations typically Chinese and the large plantations—accounting for three-fifths of the estate acreage—European-owned. Despite governmental encouragement, not too many Malays have shown the ambition and enterprise, or have been able to command the capital and management skills, to expand their holdings to larger size.

Rubber production grew an average of 3.2% per annum between 1960 and 1965 and is projected to climb 6.6% per annum between 1966 and 1970, as a result of the heavy replanting with high-yield varieties in recent years. On the whole, the record of rubber development in Malaysia suggests that an alert and enterprising population will take advantage of the available opportunities if government can provide the right conditions and atmosphere, and some encouragement for expansion. Natural rubber competes in the market under heavy obstacles, caused by the emergence and progress of synthetics, which can be and largely are being produced in the consuming countries. Technical advance in synthetics has resulted in a steady price decline and reduced the profit potential for rubber. Nevertheless, Malaysia's rubber growers, small and large, have been able to meet the challenge without a resort to massive government intervention or to nationalization, both of which have proved detrimental in other countries.

The oil palm has been commercially planted in Malaya since 1917, mostly on estates. Its recent rapid development was helped by the political trouble and government takeover in competing Indonesia and the Congo. It is now more profitable than rubber, and a major part of the new jungle clearings is used for oil palm rather than rubber planting wherever the soil quality is adequate. The tree starts to bear within three years of planting and yields continuously in about seven-day harvests until the tree's height and the cost of harvesting make replanting desirable.

Other commerical crops, such as coconut, cocoa, hemp, pepper, pineapples, tea, and tobacco, are also gaining and promise to help diversify the Malaysian economy. Timber has become the country's third most important product, after rubber and tin.

Malaysia's leading subsistence crop, rice, is not produced in quantities adequate to meet the demand of a rapidly expanding population. At least one-third of the rice is now imported —about 400,000 tons annually at a cost of U.S. $75 million— which is an unnecessary drain on foreign exchange earnings. Strengthened rice cultivation offers an opportunity for substantial savings and provides work for the rural unemployed or underemployed. Some progress has been made through the use of high-yielding varieties, fertilizer, and irrigation. In its 1966 report the National Bank of Malaysia said hopefully that "self-sufficiency is not beyond the realm of practical achievement." But the country has yet a long way to go toward this goal.

In contrast to many countries with comprehensive multi-year plans which channel a major share of their public investment into industrial plants, Malaysia's five-year plan allocates the greater part of public development funds to rural progress, and specifically to agriculture. The government focuses particularly on the promotion of drainage and irrigation schemes, the opening of suitable jungle and swamp areas to settlement and cultivation, and the spread of better farming methods.

Tin has been mined in Malaya, in a small way, for centuries. It was not until the third and fourth quarters of the nineteenth century, when waves of Chinese immigrants were attracted to the peninsula, that the number of mines and their output multiplied and Malaya gained the lead in world tin production. It now produces over two-fifths of the world supply. As in the case of rubber and other products, the industry was developed by foreigners—mostly Chinese, with Europeans coming in later, principally on large-scale operations.

Most Malaysian tin is found in placer or alluvial deposits

of cassiterite, and it is mined mainly through surface operations by gravel pumps or dredges and hydraulic sluicing. This is also true in Africa, while in Bolivia, the other major source, tin is mined at the lode site, by drilling inside deep mine shafts at high altitudes.

Chinese mining operations tend to employ gravel pumps, while the huge dredges which have come into wider use in recent years, and which require heavy economic investment, are mainly employed by European companies.

Tin mining was under restraint for many years because of limitations imposed by the International Tin Cartel, established in 1931 to hold price fluctuations within a narrow range. When tin prices fell below $1 per pound in the early 1950's, marketing quotas were cut back sharply and production restricted. Countries that depend heavily on tin for employment, governmental revenues, or foreign exchange earnings, were in trouble. But subsequent political ills in some of those countries helped to reverse the downward trend in tin prices.

Bolivia is the world's second largest tin producer. After the victory of the 1952 revolution—the country's 70th and its bloodiest—the MNR[2] party which assumed power nationalized, as it had promised, the three major tin companies which had long been the country's main source of support, and turned property and management over to a government corporation, Comibol. Mining profits, Bolivia's people were promised, would no longer flow into private pockets but would henceforth be used to finance vast development schemes and to modernize the country. As it happened, and not surprisingly, the mine work force was sharply enlarged; costs multiplied but tin output took a tailspin. Instead of profits, Comibol produced huge deficits, and tin mining turned from being the government budget's main support to become

[2] Movimiento Nacionalista Revolucionario.

a big drain. This further accelerated runaway inflation, which reduced the peso's value (originally one U.S. dollar) from one cent U.S. to less than one-hundredth of one cent by 1956. Bolivians were starving and the country was kept going only by substantial U.S. aid.

The problem, as the thorough report of an American consulting firm explained a few years later, was not technical but political: the new mine management was unable to cope with the situation in the political atmosphere in which it had to operate. Nor did conditions improve, in spite of promises renewed year after year, because the Bolivian government was unwilling—and, caught in the trap of its promises, to some extent unable—to carry out the recommendations of the mining report and its other advisors.[3]

Some other tin-producing countries had similar unfavorable experiences. Indonesia's government in 1958-60 took over the Dutch-owned tin mines with disastrous results. In the Congo, trouble started with independence in 1960 and led to open warfare and invasion.

The sharp decline in tin output by one-third to one-half in three major tin-producing countries, Bolivia, Indonesia and the Congo, eventually led to rising tin prices, which reached a high of $2.18 per pound in 1964. Malaysia increased its output, as did Thailand and a few other countries, though not sufficiently to meet the demand.

Had tin been irreplaceable its price might have climbed even higher or remained at record levels. But the high price led to a search for and development of substitutes.

Because tin is largely used as a corrosion preventive on steel cans, its excessive cost encouraged wider use of cardboard, glass, and plastic containers; stainless steel plating;

---

[3] I served at the time as fiscal advisor to the Government of Bolivia on a joint U.S. Treasury-State Department-CIA mission and as a member of the Stabilization Council, chaired by the President of the Republic.

aluminum, etc. So, not surprisingly, tin prices started sliding again, to about $1.75 in 1965 and to $1.51 in the summer of 1967. It is the genius of the market that whenever something gets out of kilter—more often than not because of governmental interference for political purposes—it finds its own corrective or, if prevented from doing so, "kicks back" in a way that is rather painful. If the powers that be recognize the cause of their distress and remedy their actions the situation may soon be self-correcting. But if they persist and redouble their efforts to make the market conform to their wishes, distress may well turn into disaster—and loud clamor for foreign aid to assuage it will ensue.

Since substitutes can replace tin in some of its uses but not in all (at least at the present time), demand for tin is likely to remain high. However, in Malaysia, as in some of the other countries, the metal content of the ore in the producing areas is declining, which, in spite of technological progress, pushes production costs upward. Though ores of lower metal content can now be processed more economically than was possible some decades ago, it is likely that tin production in Malaysia will gradually decline.

No major new finds of tin deposits have been made in Malaysia since the end of World War II. This fact, and the shaky outlook for natural rubber, largely because of growing use of synthetics, make Malaysia's heavy dependence on rubber and tin a matter of grave concern. But even if the two products were to show further growth for some years, it is unlikely that they could expand at a rate at which Malaysia's import needs, and thus requirements for foreign exchange, will climb.

Few minerals besides tin have been found in Malaysia. Iron deposits were developed by Japanese interests in 1921 and are producing, mostly for export to Japan. But the known reserves are limited and prospects for increasing the output are not favorable. Nor does bauxite, which is being mined in several locations, offer great hopes.

Great efforts have been expended in the search for petroleum. The Shell Oil Company is said to have spent close to $50 million on exploration in Malaysia, but aside from small wells in Sarawak, the search has so far been in vain. The proximity of the rich Sumatra fields rekindles interest in the Straits area from time to time, and there is hope that some day worthwhile deposits may be found. Meanwhile all electric energy must be generated from imported oil or from the limited hydroelectric sources.

MANUFACTURING INDUSTRIES

With the available mineral and exportable agricultural resources limited and the future of some of the natural products uncertain, it is not surprising that Malaysia's economic planners look to manufacturing industries as an important means of lifting the country to higher levels of prosperity. Many of the "developing countries" devote disproportionate attention—and resources—to industrial growth, for economic as well as prestige reasons, sometimes shooting for unrealistic goals at the expense of other more urgent and potentially more productive pursuits.

The industrial targets of the First Malaysia Plan (1966-70) appear moderate and reasonable and seem quite capable of fulfillment. In contrast to plans in many other new countries, this plan (like its predecessors, the earlier two Malaya five-year plans) does not propose to invest public funds in industry or to direct industrial development. Malaya's second five-year plan (1956-60) expressed the policy well:

For the future the importance of manufacturing to the Federation's long-run development and economic diversification can hardly be overemphasized. It is the policy of the government to rely on private initiative for this development, but at the same time to encourage the growth of private industry through every reasonable means of assistance, consistent with the general interest. The response from the private sector to this policy has been a matter of considerable satisfaction.

Perhaps the basic contribution that Government can make to industrial growth is the preservation of a sound and stable monetary and financial climate, free from all the restrictions, controls, and uncertainties which are the inevitable accompaniments of financial instability and inflation.

In the First Malaysia Plan (1966-70) the government reaffirms its policy of nonintervention, extends a welcome mat to "foreign entrepreneurship and capital in Malaysia's industrial development," assuring that "foreign entrepreneurs will be accorded the same incentives as local industrialists" and will, for all practical purposes, have an unrestricted right to repatriation of capital, profits, and dividends. This contrasts favorably with the attitude of many other governments, which regard foreign investors and entrepreneurs as exploiters, use them as whipping boys in their public utterances (intended to impress local constituents), and treat them accordingly.

When American or other Western capitalists show an understandable reluctance to increase their investment in certain countries or initiate new ventures which the local government wishes to be undertaken, this is taken as proof that private action cannot possibly fill the bill and that government-to-government aid is essential. As one writer observed, to offer inducements and encouragement to foreign capital is like "holding open the door of a bird cage in the expectation that more birds will fly in than out." [4]

[4] J. J. Puthucheary, *Ownership and Control in the Malaysian Economy*, Eastern Universities Press, Singapore, 1960, p. 1959.

Most of the huge Western investments in less developed countries were made voluntarily in the expectation of earning a profit. Only when and where the political climate grew frigid and the owners or managers had reason to fear that—to stay with Mr. Puthucheary's metaphor—this would truly turn into a bird cage with closed doors, were further investments stopped and attempts made to rescue capital before ambitious local politicians could claim it as their rightful spoils.

In Malaysia, as contrasted with Indonesia and other countries, no open season on foreign investors was declared, nor has the word "profit" become a dirty word. The government has concentrated on creating an environment or "climate" in which the private entrepreneur would feel comfortable, with, on the whole, gratifying results. In a story captioned "Malaysia: Investor's Magnet," *U.S. News and World Report* (February 13, 1967) reported, for example, that in one recent month 35 American firms sought entry to the Malaysian market, that a large American company had bought timber rights to some 565,000 acres in Sabah and that, of some 140 joint ventures valued at $335 million, nearly two-thirds had come from foreign sources. "Banking and economic experts are calling Malaysia 'a very good credit risk.'" Not many of the newly independent countries are so rated.

However, the split with Singapore (which cut the size of the local market), restrictions by the British and other governments, and the uncertainty about political stability in the Southeast Asia region have had a dampening effect on the prospects for increased private foreign investment in Malaysia in the second half of the 1960's. In the long range though, the outlook is definitely encouraging.

In Malaysia's economic history it is probably less important what the government did than what it did *not* do—which makes the description of economic policy much less dramatic for Malaysia than for some other more "activist" countries. When those countries had scared off would-be foreign investors, they took the resultant reluctance to invest as proof that it was useless to try to attract foreign capital, and that government-to-government aid was the only effective means of meeting capital needs of less developed countries. More often than not, the United States obliged, and provided large sums, totalling in the billions, to make up for the failure of national governments to make investment in their countries attractive to capitalists.

For some years, most of the U.S. aid has been going to countries with a mixed economy, with socialist leanings and with centralized economic planning. Malaysia was not among the benefited nations. The First Malaysia Plan (1966-70) envisaged for the first time foreign governmental aid to the extent of U.S. $630 million over the five-year period, more than half of it in loans and the rest in grants. Great Britain declined to participate, partly because of its own difficulties, and partly because the Labour government never viewed Malaysia's adherence to free enterprise with favor. Malaysia's government approached the United States in regard to aid, but the extent of any forthcoming U.S. aid is still uncertain as of this writing.

The Malaysian government's nonintervention policy has been criticized by some of its Western advisers and observers. They felt that the government ought to play an active role in industrial promotion instead of waiting for entrepreneurs to do it. "A much better way out of the dilemma would be a policy of developing public enterprise as a vehicle for industrialization," wrote Australian economist E. L. Wheelwright in *Industrialization in Malaysia* (Melbourne University Press, 1965, p. 111). "Such enterprises would be publicly owned in the same way as the Central Electricity Board and the Malayan Railways, and income from such publicly owned assets would flow into the collective purse."

The Malaysian government has so far given no sign that it

intends to follow such advice or the example of some of its neighbors and other new countries. Manufacturing, under private auspices, has been expanding at a satisfactory rate—an average of 11% per year between 1960 and 1965, which far exceeds the 4% expansion rate of agriculture, forestry, fishing and mining, and the 6.3% rate of total gross domestic product. Gross fixed investment outlays in machinery and equipment, mostly private, have tripled in the past ten years, climbing from U.S. $41 million in 1955, to U.S. $85 million in 1960, to U.S. $136 million in 1965. Industry's share in the national product increased from 9% to 11% in the 1960's, and in the employed labor force to 6%. These are still very low rates compared with those of many countries which are either more developed or have used forced-draft methods. However, it has been achieved without foreign aid and without inflation or other disrupting trends, and it shows all signs of continuing upwards.

Malaysia has been using multi-year plans which in the 1960's were prepared in the Economic Planning Unit of the Prime Minister's Department. The first two Malaya plans (1956-60 and 1961-65) have been followed by the First Malaysia Plan (1966-70), which is presently in effect. But such planning is not at all comparable to the five-year plans of India and many other countries in which government has assumed the command post of the entire economy. Malaysia's "indicative" plans are more in the nature of estimates or projections of likely developments in population and the economy, on the basis of which political and administrative officials can judge the needs for public services, roads and other means of communication, schools, and many other public services and facilities, and draw budgets accordingly.

Malaysia's government has been acutely aware of the limitations and dangers of the country's excessive dependence on rubber and tin, which now account for 55% of all exports and

30% of the gross national product. The First Malaysia Plan recognized this:

> The conclusion must be faced, therefore, that over the next five years export growth will be inadequate to finance import needs and maintain overall economic growth, even after allowance is made for export promotion and diversification.

The Plan saw the most promising solution in industrial expansion, but specified:

> As in the past, responsibility for manufacturing operations themselves will be left to the private sector. The government's role will be to maintain a favorable investment climate; to provide industrial estates [i.e., land to be used for industrial parks] and transport, power and communications facilities; and to grant tax and other inducements.

The oldest industrial operations are in the processing of the country's major natural products. This activity includes the smelting of tin ores, milling of rubber and palm oil, and processing of latex and copra; tea factories; tanning, etc. Next comes the manufacturing of consumer goods from the processed raw materials: automobile and bicycle tires, and other rubber products such as footwear; tin plating, and iron and tin goods; hardwood and plywood furniture; food and beverages; fruit canning; leather goods, etc. If produced for export purposes, these items face stiff competition, particularly in and from industrial countries, because on the whole it is more economical to produce consumer goods close to the point of consumption. Only specialized or unique items have much chance to succeed. At this time, consumer and intermediate goods account for 70% of the total manufacturing output on the Malay Peninsula, processing of agricultural products such as rubber, rice, copra, palm oil, and tea for another 20%, and the manufacturing of such capital goods as machinery, transport equipment, and other metal goods for the remaining 10%.

The manufacture of consumer goods for the local market has been making progress. In recent years about 60% of manufactured items sold in Malaysia were imported, a figure which suggests many opportunities for new enterprises, added employment, and foreign exchange savings. In recent years, manufacture of hundreds of consumer goods (and also of some industrial items) has been started or expanded—particularly rubber, leather, and textile goods; chemical, paper, and wood products; soap; cigarettes; and a variety of foods. Import substitution has become one of the most promising avenues for economic development. "In 1960 all imports of petroleum fuels entered in product form; by 1964 only 41% entered as petroleum products, while the remaining 59% entered as crude petroleum for domestic refining" (from the Deputy Prime Minister Tun Abdul Razak's speech in the House of Representatives on December 15, 1965, moving the adoption of the First Malaysia Plan). As long as large quantities of rice and other foods are imported, expansion of local production offers a great potential for improving the balance of payments, and much progress has been made in that direction.

New products often need tariff protection, at least for a limited time, and the Malaysian government has found it necessary to boost some customs rates substantially. While from a viewpoint of expanding international trade the raising of tariff walls may seem undesirable, it has proven indispensable in a world of more than one hundred nations, each trying to promote its local industries. It may be well to remember that the United States throughout the nineteenth, and much of the twentieth, century offered its industries ample protection by high tariff rates.

The prospects of developing a broad domestic market were sharply reduced when Singapore was separated from Malaysia in August 1965 and formed an independent republic. Plans to lower tariffs between Singapore and Malaya have been abandoned, and each country has been trying to protect its own industries ever since. Some factories which had been planned to supply the markets of Malaysia and Singapore, and which were then cut off from one or the other by prohibitive customs rates, were hard hit. This shrinkage in the size of the potential market darkens the outlook for developing a strong industrial complex. For some products which call for large-scale operations, local manufacture may no longer be economical. But the split is a reality, and a reunion is not likely to materialize for many hears ahead.

SOCIALISM IN SINGAPORE?

When the state of Singapore was about to obtain its independence from the British Crown in 1963, it was widely believed that the island city of 224 square miles, crowded by almost two million people, would not by itself be able to form a viable country. To soften the impact of adding nearly 1½ million Chinese to Malaya's population, two territories in Northern Borneo, Sabah and Sarawak, were also brought in to form the new country of Malaysia. But the merger still meant that there were about as many Chinese in Malaysia as Malays. Because the Chinese were far more active in the modern sectors of the economy, the political union seemed to lead to a Chinese predominance, which proved unacceptable to Malaya's indigenous inhabitants, the Malays. Conflicts multiplied, and a divorce became inevitable within two years.

Not long after Singapore formed a republic, on August 9, 1965, it became apparent that not only could it exist on its own but this tiny island with a population density of over 80,000 per square mile, entirely devoid of natural resources (even its water is imported in pipes across the Straits of Johore), was doing very well indeed. As the leading *entrepôt*, a center of trade and finance for a vast area, with a GNP approaching $1 billion and a per-capita income exceeding $500, occupied by a population of unbending energy and ambition with a wide array of skills, Singapore faces a brighter future than most observers expected.

Though almost four-fifths Chinese, Singapore does not want to be, as it has been called, a "Third China." It chose Malay as its official language, and a Malay and Muslim as its head of state. English is the language of its administration, courts, and big business. But the government is run firmly and effectively by a brilliant Chinese lawyer and former union official, Lee Kuan Yew.

Singapore's government is officially labeled socialist, and Mr. Lee himself has a long background of activity much to the left of the political center. Yet it is hard to conceive of a country whose economic policies are more decisively grounded in *laissez-faire*, and whose government leaves the economy more clearly to private enterprise, free and untrammeled by limitations, restrictions, or controls. This is strange socialism, indeed.

In a speech on August 25, 1966, to the General Printing Workers' Union, whose legal adviser he had been for many years, Prime Minister Lee revealed to his former brethren and comrades what change had come over him and why. It had been charged, he said, that after a lifetime of working for the organized working-class movement he had suddenly decided "to become anti-labour, anti-treble pay, anti-the-worker."

He reminded his listeners that in the old days he had urged

them to demand treble pay and to work less. "But I know, and more and more every year I know, that in many fields it is wrong."

Mr. Lee told his audience, in response to sharp criticism of his policies by trade-union leaders, that

> ... if we repose the destiny of our people in the hands of people with a great deal of working-class loyalty, patriotism, working-class enthusiasm, with a desire to create a more just and equal society but with a singular lack of the knowledge of what makes an economy tick, what makes a society flourish; if we repose our destiny in the hands of the people who issue statements I have been reading, then I say, gentlemen, wipe off your future, because nobody is going to have any confidence in this place and this place will not tick on the basis of slogans.

He made it clear that he favored a system "in which you make it worth a man's while to work hard," i.e., a system of pay based on production results.

With much of the contemporary Chinese literature being produced in mainland China, Mr. Lee is aware of the steady Red propaganda that is being showered upon Singapore's citizens, glamorizing the virtues of communism and socialism. But he promised that

> ... as we educated the population on the stupidities of the communist creed, so we will educate the population on the stupidities of outdated, outmoded ideas, and we will introduce and inject into our population new, vigorous ideas that will ensure our survival.

To be sure, Singapore's government engages in many extensive welfare activities, such as the building of schools and health facilities. Its Housing Development Board (HDB) manages over 70,000 public housing units and adds another

10,000 to 12,000 each year. About 430,000 people, more than a fifth of Singapore's population, are now publicly housed, mostly in one- to three-room flats in huge apartment blocks. Because of a small government subsidy they pay rents averaging from $8 to $15 a month, which is slightly cheaper than private accommodations would be. But the pursuit of the industrial and commercial activities which sustain the republic's two million people is entirely in private hands. Small wonder that leaders of Singapore's *Barisan Socialis* (Socialist Front) have charged Prime Minister Lee with being in league with "colonialists, imperialists, and fascists."

Singapore's former Finance Minister, now Defense Minister, Dr. Goh Keng Swee, in an address before the Malayan Economic Society on July 24, 1966, pointed at the rapid progress in Malaysia and Singapore, "which are developing at a fair rate and which may, in a few decades, achieve the same standards of living as Western Europe [enjoys] today, as a refutation of the view that democracy is incompatible with fast development in backward countries." He ridiculed the general use of such euphemisms as "underdeveloped," popular in the 1950's, and "developing" countries, popular in the 1960's, and heaped scorn upon the taboo that kept people from frankly talking about "the poor and backward countries of Asia and Africa."

The 1960's, he said, were turning into a "Decade of Disenchantment" because the politicians in those countries did not understand (nor did they want to understand) the economics of development, but preferred to engage in "magic incantations" and a method which "resembles the mental approach with which the primitive tribesman tries to overcome his private misfortune."

Dr. Goh questioned the belief that capital investment by itself is the source and foundation of economic growth, and expressed his conviction that the secret of rapid advance lies in a policy of economic freedom. But, he concluded, governments of backward Asian and African countries continue to copy the communist folly of centralized planning and control over the economy: "to proliferate controls, licensing systems, and directions and decrees in an ever increasing torrent."

Singapore's prosperity is not without clouds or challenges. Most of the countries it serves as a trade center are trying to establish their own commercial and financial facilities, to deal directly with producers and with overseas and local customers, and to eliminate the middleman. To protect its future, Singapore has for some years been trying to build up an industrial basis in order to reduce its lopsided dependence on international trade, which may become dangerous as the sophistication of neighboring countries advances. The government set aside a 15,000-acre site on the island's southwest coast for an industrial park and later, for residential extension. About 2,600 acres were cleared of jungle and swamps, and have been occupied by a variety of industrial plants. Work is under way for a 3,000-acre expansion. The government built deepwater wharves, good road and rail connections, and other essential facilities, and offered long-term leases at the Jurong Industrial Center in addition to two-year to five-year tax exemptions and other concessions to "pioneer industries."

Shipyards had long been an important industry, and many types of manufacturing were now added: fabrication of iron products ranging from steel bars, sheets, and pipes to zippers; aluminum rolling; chemical, plastic, textile and garment, veneer and plywood plants; sugar and petroleum refineries; flour mills; and automobile and electric appliance assemblies. In Singapore today, well over 2,000 industrial establishments are operating, in which more than $300 million of private capital were invested in the 1960's, largely from domestic sources, but much of it from Japan, the United States, Australia, and Western European countries. Most of the output is intended for local consumption, but a sizeable share aims at export, as stressed in Singapore's Second Development Plan (1966-70).

The separation of Singapore and Malaysia in 1965 and the subsequent tariff boosts in both countries reduced the size of the market for industrial and consumer products in each, thus eliminating many marginal items and potential manufactures which could no longer compete across the customs barrier. It cut into the output of existing companies, and lessened attraction to foreign investors and entrepreneurs. But it also strengthened the determination on both sides to produce needed goods locally, although on a smaller scale and in smaller plants.

The withdrawal of all British forces east of Suez within the next few years, as announced in 1967, and the threatened closing of its big naval base will deal Singapore a heavy blow. It will not be easy to replace the lost income.

MALAYA'S INDUSTRIAL ESTATES

Malaya founded in 1952 a model town a few miles north of Kuala Lumpur, named Petaling Jaya, to which, a few years later, an industrial park was added. The 4,000-acre site now supports close to 60,000 inhabitants and about 150 plants. The government cleared the jungle and built roads and other communications, schools, utilities (water, sewer, electric power), and public administration buildings.

It also provided encouragement, technical aid, and credit to would-be entrepreneurs through the Malayan Industrial Development Finance, Ltd. (MIDFL)—whose creation had been recommended by the International Bank for Reconstruction and Development (IBRD)—and through several other public instrumentalities. But the development of the community was left to private initiative and private interests.

A visit to the model town of Petaling Jaya is a most pleasant and encouraging experience. One would have to go a long way from there to find anything more closely resembling an American suburb than Petaling Jaya's residential sections, schools, movie theaters, and shops. On a central hill are the modern government administration buildings whose rooftops afford a sweeping view of the city all the way to the rapidly growing University of Malaya. Several government offices are located here—only a few miles from the capital of Kuala Lumpur. The National Productivity Center, suggested by the U.N. a few years ago, aims to educate technical and professional personnel and future managers through such courses in industrial and commercial skills as industrial engineering, management accounting, etc. Its staffing is typical of many Malaysian public offices; an enthusiastic Malay, Abu Kassim, heads it, backed up by an assistant of Chinese descent, Yip Phooi Thong. In some offices, such as that of the Economic Planning Unit in the Prime Minister's department, positions are reversed: the chief is a Chinese, his assistant a Malay.

Facing the government complex is the shopping district, and some distance away a 736-acre industrial park. A four-lane expressway connects the park with the town center and with the highway to Kuala Lumpur, the airport, and Port Swettenham, Malaysia's primary seaport. Petaling Jaya's industrial park is now fully occupied, and similar estates have been started in the south, in Johore state, and near Ipoh in the north.

Several hundred products are being manufactured at Petaling Jaya, ranging from air-conditioning units to perfumes and baby powder, and from pharmaceuticals to cigarettes and batteries. Many of the companies and much of the capital and technical know-how come from the United States, Australia, Britain, Canada, Japan, and other countries, but a substantial share is of local origin. Under an ordinance of 1958, the government offers new industries "pioneer status," which grants freedom from income taxes for up to five years, freedom from customs duties on equipment, remission of duties on raw materials for export products, liberalized depreciation, etc.

At the end of 1966, 109 pioneer companies were operating in West Malaysia, i.e., the Malay Peninsula, with a capital investment of $112 million (more than half foreign-supplied), 12,000 employees, and a net annual production of $55 million. Twenty-nine of the companies manufacture chemical and petroleum products, 25 metal and engineering goods, 18 food and beverages, and 37 other goods, including textile, clothing, wood and rattan products.

Dunlop Tire is Petaling Jaya's largest factory, but there are many other sizeable plants, including branch operations of such well known American firms as Johnson & Johnson, Warner-Lambert, Colgate-Palmolive, Carrier, and Singer Sewing Machines.

Industrial managers in Malaya generally are quite happy with the conditions under which they operate (which is not true in several other South Asian countries), although some are concerned about the reduction in their market by Singapore's separation. There are prospects for relief of this reduction. At a meeting in Manila in September 1966, representatives of the three original members of the Association of Southeast Asia (ASA)—Malaysia, the Philippines, and Thailand—laid the groundwork for economic cooperation that may lead to the creation of a Southeast Asian, and eventually a South Asian, common market.

Malaysia does not formally require a majority share for Malaysians, or in fact any participation by nationals, in the ownership of new or expanded enterprises established by foreign corporations. However, as in all other less developed countries, the government prefers, and strongly suggests, that participation by local citizens in the capital structure, in management, and in the professional work force is desirable and in the interest of the sponsoring company. The term "strongly suggests" may be an understatement. Invariably, there is pressure brought to hire and train Malaysians for executive, supervisory, foremen's, technical, and other specialized openings, and for a gradual replacement of foreigners by local citizens. In the case of companies granted "pioneer" status, this becomes a requirement.

A "pioneer" certificate awarded to a company by the Minister of Commerce and Industry may, for example, stipulate "that no less than 70% of the capital of the company shall be subscribed and held by Federal citizens," "that the company shall employ and train Federal citizens in executive and technical appointments up to managerial level," "that the number of foreign personnel to be engaged and their respective periods of engagement by the company must have the prior written approval of this Ministry," "that a realistic training program of Federal citizens shall be carried out by the company so that the withdrawal of foreign personnel shall be implemented within the period approved by the Government," and that a specified percentage of the output shall be exported. There may also be a provision that the payment of royalties, technical assistance fees, etc., shall be subject to prior approval of the Ministry.

In actual practice, companies often experience great difficulty in getting approval for the hiring of foreign personnel, and they find that the authorities tend to reduce the number of foreign technicians or managers they can employ and to cut the length of their contracts or withdraw their visas, even when satisfactory replacement is not available locally. This policy is not peculiar to Malaysia; it is typical of most countries. However, foreign companies are not likely to be eager to invest their money, to establish or expand operations, when their control over their own personnel—hiring, firing, promotion, and conferral of responsibility—is limited, and when they cannot select for important or sensitive posts employees of established confidence whose first loyalty lies with the company with which they have found their career prospects and future.

Indeed, Malaysia's national policy goes beyond requiring a minimum participation of Malaysian citizens in the ownership and work force of an enterprise. It distinguishes between various ethnic groups, and may, for example, specify that at least 20% of the capital and 50% of the jobs *at all grades* shall be reserved for *Malays*—to the exclusion of Malaysian citizens of Chinese, Indian, European, or other ancestry. This brings us to the most serious and most ominous problem of Malaysia, which, unless satisfactorily resolved, could jeopardize its otherwise bright future, and which needs to be discussed in greater detail: the Malay-Chinese problem.

THE MALAY-CHINESE PROBLEM IN MALAYSIA

The indigenous population of the Malay Peninsula and of the islands of Indonesia is of Malay stock.[5] Among the people, local variations in language, customs or attitudes developed during centuries of Dutch domination over the islands and nominal independence under local sultans with British "protection" (i.e., control) on the peninsula, but these differences are minor. About 800,000 Indians and Pakistanis now live in

---

[5] The ethnic composition of Malaysia is as follows:
(1966 estimates)

Malay	4,528,000	48.2%
Chinese	3,341,000	35.6
Indian and Pakistani	899,000	9.6
Other	620,000	6.6
	9,388,000	100.0%

Malaysia, and persons of Chinese descent number some 3.3 million, comprising about one-fourth of the more than 13 million overseas Chinese who reside in the countries of Southeast Asia.[6] In Malaysia, as elsewhere, the Chinese play a far more important role in society than their share of the entire population (36% at the present time) would suggest. They dominate the modern sectors of the economy—trade, industry, finance, professions, mining, plantations (except for a limited number of large units under European control)—and leave to the Malays their traditional occupations: small-scale agriculture, fishing, and forestry.

The cause of this uneven development appears obvious to a visitor: the Malays live now, and have for centuries lived, in a benevolent environment whose abundance grants them the essentials of livelihood without an excessive struggle. They have inherited an easy-going, friendly, conservative temperament, and most Malays have displayed little ambition to engage in intensive commercial-industrial activities and in modern, competitive entrepreneurship. They call themselves *Bumiputras*—Sons of the Earth—and, with the exception of the ruling elite and military families, tend to be peasants not only by occupation but seemingly by inclination. The great majority show little interest in becoming wage earners, much less hard-driving businessmen.

The presence of an ambitious and economically highly competent minority in the midst of a less intense and economically less effective majority tends to create severe tensions which, if permitted to accumulate, may lead to disturbances

[6] Many residents of Chinese descent who have lived in Malaysia, Indonesia, Thailand and neighboring lands for one or more generations regard themselves no longer as overseas Chinese but as nationals of the countries of their residence, and are making genuine attempts at assimilation. This is particularly true of those connected with their respective governments. Policies of the Peking government have contributed to the alienation of many who formerly maintained allegiance to and communications with mainland China.

and violence.[7] This is just what happened in the case of the Armenians in Turkey and of the Jews in several European and non-European countries. Similarly, the Indians and Pakistanis in Eastern Africa, the Indians in Fiji,[8] and Europeans in several less developed countries make these areas other potential conflict arenas. The threat is no less serious when the roles are reversed—that is, when the economically less successful but sizeable ethnic group is in the minority, such as the Negroes in the United States. In either case the situation is emotionally charged and lends itself to political exploitation which may result in mob action.

In the middle of the nineteenth century, Chinese immigrants to Malaya began to explore, develop, and man tin mines and rubber plantations. Coolies were imported for about the same reason for which Negroes were brought to the Americas: the indigenous population was disinclined and seemed unsuited to do the type of work which the developers deemed necessary. The Chinese came as indentured labor (a practice abolished only in 1914) under conditions which in some respects resembled those of African slaves shipped to the Western Hemisphere for work on Southern U.S. and Brazilian plantations. But the Chinese coolies in Southeast Asia developed none of the characteristics which are sometimes said to be the results of living under slavery or near-slavery conditions. To be sure, many of the descendants of the coolies of the 1850's or early 1900's are still at the bottom rung of the socio-economic ladder, eking out a bare existence through menial labor. But the more able and ambitious among the Chinese mastered the obstacles that faced them and over-

[7] There have been incidents such as the disturbances at Penang, but so far they have not assumed serious dimensions.

[8] The Indians now probably constitute a slight majority of Fiji's population, but so long as Fijians compose the armed forces and (with British help) maintain effective control of the government, the situation is almost as if the Indians were a minority.

came the distinct animosity that surrounded them. When they found that they had little chance to compete with the Malays in certain occupations, such as the civil service, the army or police, they concentrated on filling the gap which the Malays had left: development of the industrial and service sector essential to a twentieth-century economy, as entrepreneurs, investors, managers, technicians, operators, and common laborers. Today many of the positions in the higher ranks (particularly since the gradual withdrawal of many European expatriates) and most of the jobs in the middle ranks—accountants, clerks, mechanics, craftsmen—are filled by persons of Chinese descent, and one may walk through the offices of many companies, large and small, without seeing more than a scattering of Malay faces.

Many of the banking, insurance, shipping, wholesale, and industrial companies have long been trying to hire Malays for white collar jobs, and also for blue collar jobs, either on their own volition or under governmental and public pressure. On the whole, they have had little success. Only business firms willing to apply lower standards of employment and promotion to Malays than to others have been able to hire or advance a significant number. That such a situation leads to more than just isolated cases of discontent, Americans have painfully learned in recent years.

In Malaysia, as almost everywhere else in the world, the Chinese maintain segregation in large or small Chinatowns in regard to housing, education (schools), social life (clubs and associations), politics, economic activity, etc. To some extent immigrants almost everywhere band together—as New York has shown—to form communities for mutual protection in a hostile climate. But the Chinese have on the whole done a more thorough job of this; they are a nation with the proud heritage of an old and high civilization which traditionally has looked at all other people as barbarians. Chinese immigration ceased before World War II, so that all of the younger people are now native citizens of Malaysia, a fact which so far has changed their attitude only slightly. Parental influence and tradition are still strong.

In Malaysia's constitution, Article 8(2) establishes the principle of nondiscrimination because of religion, race, descent, or place of birth, but, as in most other countries, theory and practice do not always coincide. Suffrage, however, is on the whole on a one-man one-vote basis. But, for example, a 1962 amendment enables rural voters to choose half the number of electors in urban contituencies. Since Malays are largely rural, Chinese mostly urban, this grants Malays a stronger representation.

The University of Malaya applies decidedly lower standards of admission to applicants of Malay extraction.[9] Most scholarships go to Malay students, and many young Chinese find it difficult to raise enough money to pay for their education. Tuition amounts to $110 per quarter (10 weeks), room and board to $50, which is a great deal of money in a country whose per-capita income equals only one-tenth of the U.S. level. The annual cost of education at the University of Malaya, the major state institution, runs, on a comparative-income basis, much higher than at the most expensive private universities in the United States.

Even so, better than two-thirds of the students at the University of Malaya are of Chinese descent. Most Malays who attend the university enroll in what is called "Malayan studies," regarded by students as breeze courses which enable them to acquire sufficient credits for graduation. All students at the engineering college, and all but two at the College of

---

[9] This is similar to the practice of many American universities and colleges that wish to have a greater Negro representation, and to the policies of some European universities which used to apply a "numerus clausus" to the admission of Jewish students.

SOCIALISM AND PRIVATE ENTERPRISE

50

Science, are Chinese. Of 183 Bachelor of Science degrees awarded in June 1966, 160 went to Chinese students, 18 to Indians, and only five to Malays. Even in agricultural science only two degrees were earned by Malays.

When in September 1966 the Deputy Prime Minister announced that the MARA College [10] would for the first time be open to non-Malay students, the Institute for Malay Participation in Commerce and Industry protested: the college, it said in a statement, had been established with the aim of training Malays and other indigenous people. The Institute feared that an "open door" policy would lead to a reduction in the number of Malay students—as in fact it had at the University of Malaya, where only a small fraction of the students now were Malays. At the Serdang Agricultural College enrollment had at one time been 70% Malay. But under an "open door" policy this had shrunk to a mere 12%.

Many Malay students attend the University of Malaya in order to qualify for good positions in the civil service. Malaya's civil service was established under British rule and enjoys a good reputation for competence. In fact, Malaysians freely attribute the high caliber of their public service to their colonial past, which citizens of other formerly dependent nations tend to denigrate and almost never credit with any desirable development or accomplishment (but which they blame for their failures and, in fact, for everything that fails to fulfill their desires or aspirations). In spite of the constitutional rule of nondiscrimination, civil-service entrance and promotion are far easier for Malays than for Chinese. Under a long-established rule the Malaysian civil service employs three Malays for every Chinese.

It is quite likely that if the university and the civil service gave no preference to Malays, the composition of their student body and work force at all levels, high and low, might

10 MARA (Majlis Amanah Ra'ayat—Institution for the Preservation of the [indigenous] People) aims to help the Malays and strengthen their position.

gradually come to resemble that of the staffs of most of the nation's business enterprises: it would be predominantly or overwhelmingly Chinese. Malay leaders are well aware of this and hang on, with firm determination and by all means, to the government services, the armed forces, and the police. Their political leaders are afraid of what would happen if the natural or market forces were permitted free play and allowed the ethnic groups to compete on equal terms: the Malays might become "red Indians" in their own country. They know that it is one thing to establish the theoretical principle of equal rights and another to practice it, when equal rights means unequal results. And what the Malays are interested in and aim for is more nearly equal results, not equal opportunity. Therefore they are convinced that, at least for the time being and certainly for a long time to come, the government must throw its weight on the side of the economically less competent—their own group—through preference in many forms. They try to maintain the appearance of "equal rights" only as long as this does not obstruct their true goal—just as we do here in the United States, as many other countries have long been doing overtly or covertly, and as most of the new countries are doing. Some governments try to explain or excuse their policy by saying that the former colonial power failed to train and educate indigenous people to assume greater responsibilities. In Malaya, however, it is obvious that the British did *not* train the Chinese while nelgecting the Malays. The Malays, as the ruling group, were always accorded preference. In Malaya as elsewhere, including the United States, many of the Chinese (in common with some other ethnic groups) lifted themselves up by their bootstraps while others did not.

Chinese holding high positions in government or in private business, to whom I talked during my stay in Malaysia, were quite anxious to assure me of their satisfaction with conditions as they are, to assert that they had no reason to complain, that

Chinese people who were willing to labor hard enough had an opportunity to rise (though they might have to work harder than Malays to achieve comparable results), that the government was doing everything in its power to be fair to ethnic minorities, that Chinese-Malay relations were gradually improving, and that harmony was, if not just around the corner, at least not too far away. "The Chinese are treated better in Malaysia than in any other country in the world."

Nevertheless, in talking with the Chinese I could not help feeling that most or all of them were deeply troubled, that they were trying to hide from me, the American visitor, their resentment, the inner fear or even terror, that gripped them. The recent slaughter in Indonesia of tens of thousands of Chinese men and women—many of them entirely unconnected with communist activities—and the continuing persecution of three million other Chinese people there were warning signs that recalled the cruel fate of economically effective minorities in Europe and other countries within the past few decades and in earlier periods of history.

It is undoubtedly true that the Malaysian government and its leaders—particularly Prime Minister Tunku Abdul Rahman and Deputy Prime Minister Tun Abdul Razak—are trying their utmost to treat all ethnic groups as fairly as possible, to reduce racial tensions, and to lead the country to a harmonious future. The Alliance Party, which, as noted, has dominated Parliament and the government since before independence, is composed of three groups which formed a close liaison representing the three major ethnic segments of the country's population: the UMNO (United Malay National Organization), MCA (Malayan Chinese Association), and MIC (Malayan Indian Congress). Its cohesion has so far stood up under heavy stress and will, it is hoped, continue to weather the attacks of agitators and extremists from both sides. The broad support for a policy of moderation and compromise among the Malaysian people is apparent from the results of the last parliamentary elections in April 1964, mentioned earlier: the Alliance Party won 125 seats out of a total of 159. It holds 240 state assembly seats out of a total of 282. But the task of reconciling nationalist feelings will not be simple, nor is it getting easier.

The growing importance of the modern sectors of the economy, industry, finance, commerce, and large-scale enterprise as such, and the inevitable *relative* decline of agriculture, as well as the continuing Malaysianization of the managerial, technical, and other work force (i.e., the gradual replacement of European personnel) tend to strengthen and accelerate the upward movement of the Chinese and to widen the economic discrepancy between them and the Malays. The income gap between Malays and Chinese does not appear to be narrowing.[11] These trends and prospects tend to feed the fires of nationalist feeling among both Malays and Chinese and to provide ammunition with which irresponsible politicians raise extreme demands and incite malcontents to violence.

All of this leaves the government in an unenviably delicate position. It cannot disregard dissatisfaction among the groups which provide much of its political power and without which it could not effectively lead the country. Nor can it afford to alienate the segments that account for much of Malaysia's dramatic economic advance, which is the envy of many of its neighbors. Above all, Malaysia's government genuinely aims to set an example of just government in a multi-racial country without undue favoritism to any one group.

All of this faces the government with a dilemma: should it intensify its war on rural poverty, intervene more forcefully on behalf of the Malays, and risk driving the Chinese into opposition—even into the hands of the communists—and so damage the country's economic prospects and national co-

[11] No statistics are available on income distribution by brackets, by ethnic groups or on a historical basis.

hesion? Or should it let nature and competition take its course and thereby fan the sails of reckless agitators and demagogues who might well gain widespread support for extreme demands among Malays?

Observers who *a priori* favor governmental over private action use this conflict to offer their methods as a solution. E. L. Wheelwright wrote in *Industrialization in Malaysia* (Melbourne University Press, 1965, pp. 110-111):

> ... a policy of industrialization which relies on indigenous private enterprise must inevitably increase the economic power of the Chinese, either in their capacity as industrial entrepreneurs, or as investing capitalists. Most of the jobs created in industry will be filled by Chinese, partly because of the method of recruitment through the Chinese extended family system, and partly because Malays lack the necessary skills, training and aptitude for industrial work in the towns. If the offtake from the countryside into the towns proceeds at a faster rate than jobs in industry become available, the Malays, unassisted, will lose in the competition for these jobs; herein lie the seeds of racial strife.

Earlier in this chapter, I cited the solution which Wheelwright suggests; but it bears repeating at this point:

> A much better way out of the dilemma would be a policy of developing public enterprise as a vehicle for industrialization. Such enterprises would be publicly owned in the same way as the Central Electricity Board and the Malayan Railways, and income from such publicly owned assets would flow into the collective purse.

Wheelwright continues:

> Also, and of great importance is the fact that they [the public enterprises] could be charged with the specific task of training

Malay managers and workers on the job, thus ensuring greater equality of opportunity in industry for Malays.

In this view, governmental ownership of the means of production would achieve two objectives: it would insure public direction of industrial development and would enable the government to do in industry what it is doing in the civil service: prefer Malays in its employment and promotion practices. The *Far Eastern Economic Review* presented a similar thought in a more restrained form in its *1966 Yearbook* (p. 229):

> ... that the Alliance [Party's] stress on private enterprise and initiative which had served Malayan development so well in the past 100 years had definite limitations when applied to the problems of rural poverty and to the dilemmas created by an uneven multi-racial distribution of wealth.

As to the rural poverty, it may be well to recall that the 1965 report of the ECAFE (p. 1) named agriculture "the least satisfactory sector of the economy" in the entire Asia-Far East region, and that Malaya's agricultural production has shown a higher rate of growth than that of any other country in the region except Thailand and Taiwan (Republic of China). The Malaysian government's favoritism toward the Malays, who are mostly rural, yielded an incidental benefit: Malaysia paid more attention to agriculture than did most other similarly situated countries, whose multi-year plans and governmental investment schemes tended to focus on glamorous types of industrial development (steel mills, airlines, etc.) at the expense of the more basic and more urgent needs of agriculture.

The policy which Mr. Wheelwright suggested—of governmental action in industrial development—would accomplish certain political and ideological objectives. The question is what it would do to the development of Malaysia's economy in years to come. Would Malaysia continue to grow economically as well or better under a system of government ownership and planned direction? The example of many other countries which have followed that path certainly does not so suggest. But, on the other hand, can we attribute past growth to the fact that the country has been applying free-enterprise principles? Success of a market or free-enterprise system depends on the existence of an energetic entrepreneur class which takes advantage of the available opportunities. Such a class exists in Malaysia—composed mostly of Chinese, Europeans, and a few Indians with some, but not many, Malays. Supposing the Chinese had not been there; would the Malays have shown the initiative to develop the tin mines, rubber plantations, commerce, finance, and industry? Or would Malaysia, with the exception of its European components, still largely be a peasant country, as backward and poor as Indonesia and many other of the new countries? Does Indonesia lag not because of its socialist policies but because it has only a small Chinese population which was (and is) repressed and never had a chance to assume the kind of economic leadership assumed by its much stronger counterpart in Malaysia?

During colonial times proportionately far more Dutchmen immigrated to the Netherlands' possessions in the East Indies (now Indonesia) than did Britishers to Malaya, to man managerial, technical, and clerical jobs.[12] The Dutch government

---

[12] There were about 250,000 Dutchmen in a population of an estimated 60 million in the Dutch East Indies just prior to World War II, about 10,000 Britishers among Malaya's 8 million; that equals 0.4% Dutchmen in Indonesia, 0.13% Britons in Malaya. Mr. R. H. Hopper, vice-president of American Overseas Petroleum Ltd., added some interesting observations in correspondence with the author: about 80% of the Dutchmen in the East Indies were Eurasians, often several generations removed from Holland. Many of the young Dutchmen who came from the Netherlands did so because they faced unemployment at home, and the East Indies was the only major Dutch possession overseas. Britons had many larger and more promising places to go than Malaya.

also engaged far more directly and extensively in the development of the country's natural assets and economic potential than did the British government in Malaya. Was this so because the Dutch leaned more toward governmental leadership and control? Or was it because they found no class of local residents able and eager to take the initiative, fill the clerical positions, provide the capital—as the British found in Malaya's Chinese? [13]

I have no definitive answer to these questions. Such answers will require the uncovering and accumulation of far more facts than I was able to gather in the short time of my visit. Some facts, however, stand out clearly: Malaysia set an outstanding example of stable economic growth in Asia, advancing to a rank second only to Japan, under a system of free private enterprise. Other countries, under tight government planning and direction, meanwhile failed to come up to expectations and sank into ever deeper trouble. This suggests that the classic principles of "the nature and causes of the wealth of nations" still apply, almost 200 years after they were first formulated by Adam Smith. It proves that they work well where the conditions are right—as they seem to have been in Malaysia. Whether they are *necessarily* successful under all conditions is another question, which cannot be answered with certainty from Malaysia's experience.

[13] Mr. Hopper suggested several reasons why many more Chinese migrated to Malaya than to Indonesia: the Malayan Peninsula is nearer to China than the Archipelago, and the British imported Chinese to Malaya as laborers. The Dutch had no need to import Chinese; the Japanese have to be good workers, coming as they do from an overpopulated area where the struggle for existence is hard.

CHAPTER III

Indonesia's Socialist Economy

An alert and observant visitor to Indonesia needs little time to become aware of the nature of the public policies which governed the country through most of the postwar period—and of the resultant status of its economic health. He may or may not suspect that there is more than an accidental connection between past policies and the present economic status. Undoubtedly he will be struck by the many incongruities he sees around him, above all by the general poverty, which contrasts so dramatically with the country's natural endowment —an endowment which makes this, one of the world's most populous lands, potentially one of its most prosperous. Certainly the atmosphere that pervades Djakarta is entirely different from that of Kuala Lumpur, although climate and people are very similar in the two capitals.

On the way from the airport to downtown Djakarta, the taxi driver is likely to offer the foreigner a black market rate for his dollar bills. A day or two later the visitor will learn the rate offered was somewhat lower than those rates which other operators quote to him. He will receive many such quotations as he makes his rounds over the wide boulevards and through the narrow streets of this city of nearly four million which for over 300 years was known as Batavia.

Having become used to the scarcity of vacant rooms and the necessity of making advance reservations in big luxury hotels throughout the Orient, the tourist will be pleasantly

59

surprised to find that there is always ample space at Djakarta's new and sumptuous Hotel Indonesia.[1] If he visits the opulent two-year-old Samudra Beach Hotel on Java's splendid south shore, the Ambarrukmo Palace Hotel in Jogjakarta, or the new Bali Beach Hotel, he is likely most of the time to find few guests.

When the visitor peers from his room at the Hotel Indonesia, he may wonder about a 40-story unfinished steel skeleton just across the square. He will soon learn that this was to be a palatial office building whose construction was halted by the new government in 1966 when money ran out, and it became obvious there would not be enough tenants to justify completion. When he asks about the gray buildings which flank the rusting steel structure and notes that they are lifeless shells, he will be told that they are the remains of the British Embassy, sacked and burned by government-instigated and government-organized mob violence in 1963.[2] Later on he may run across the U. S. Information Agency offices which suffered a similar fate.

Economic contrasts throughout Djakarta are truly striking. Two blocks beyond the Hotel Indonesia, on a splendid boulevard, stands a just-finished 14-story department store named after Sukarno's childhood nurse, Sarinah. It is crowded because Djakartans love to ride up and down its escalators, a contraption new to them. But only the lower floors are stocked, largely with imported goods which are too costly for most residents to buy. The store, which cost $14 million to build, is worlds apart from the city's other retail shops—one-story, primitive, and traditionally oriental. Nearby is an immense mosque, once envisioned as the biggest in all Islam but left less than half completed and now deserted. There are many huge, flamboyant monuments and vast ultra-modern

---

[1] This appears to be changing in 1967.
[2] The Indonesian government is repairing the damage in 1967.

ministries, surrounded by a sea of misery, by square miles of crumbling houses that reek of the squalor of endless tropical slums, dotted with a few middle-class settlements.

Ancient and magnificent palaces are found amid communities of miserable mud huts in many Asiatic countries; earlier ages took such incongruity for granted. However, in a twentieth-century city such contrasts suggest basic confusion: the authorities who ordered such projects and the planners who designed them were apparently out of touch with the community's needs and failed to take into account the economic resources and the environmental conditions needed to support such programs. Clearly they were imbued with grandiose ideas but lacked the judgment to realize them. And since the ministries and the monuments, the hotels and the department store, the mosque and the sports stadia, and virtually all of the other large projects of the last 20 years have been designed, constructed, owned, and operated by the government, it is apparent that government leaders have acted in economic ignorance and unconcern. Their actions have exacted a frightful price of suffering from the masses for whom, presumably, all this was done.

It is now generally recognized in Indonesia, as it has long been known abroad, that the Sukarno regime, which led the country to independence after World War II and then ruled it for sixteen years, bears most of the responsibility for the steady decline in its economic fortunes and for the destitution of its people. Opinions vary on specific causes, however. Were the goals and policies of the government wrong? Was merely their execution faulty? Could the plans have succeeded if their administration had been effective? If so, can failure be attributed to the personal shortcomings of the rulers, to their ignorance of economics, their foibles, inconsistencies, extravagances, impulsive actions and military ventures, to their evident inability to carry major programs through to completion?

Could Sukarno's plans have succeeded if he had proven to be as good a chief executive as he was a revolutionary leader?

Or should we seek the cause for Indonesia's decline in the goals which the government set for the country, in the type of society it intended to build, in the kind of economy it wished to create? Were the aims of the new republic, as proclaimed at its founding in 1949, and in succeeding years, unrealistic and therefore doomed to failure?

Before attempting to form even tentative answers to such questions, it may be well to describe Indonesia's land, people, and resources, for a better understanding of the forces at work.

INDONESIA'S LAND, PEOPLE, AND RESOURCES

Indonesia, the world's largest archipelago, is composed of two dozen major islands and over 3,000 smaller isles which straddle the equator and extend 3,400 miles from the northwest tip of Sumatra to the border of the Australian mandate of East New Guinea. The entire area receives abundant precipitation, ranging from 40 to 100 inches, well distributed throughout the year. There are none of those alternating drought and flood periods which are the curse of so many other lands. Indonesia has almost no seasons and enjoys more or less steady temperatures in the seventies or eighties, rarely reaching 90° or falling below 70°. Humidity, almost always high, is relieved by frequent sea breezes in coastal and mountain areas.

Dotted with volcanoes, Java, where two-thirds of Indonesia's people live, is covered with highly fertile volcanic soil which, nurtured by almost daily rains and steady heat, gives the land a perpetual growing season, with two or more crops a year and a natural fecundity paralleled in few other countries.

Java is now fully cultivated. Useful plants cover all arable land throughout the year, save for slopes on which forests must be maintained to prevent soil erosion. Some of the outer islands, however, still have vast stretches of lush primeval growth that could be put to the plow, although here the soil is not as fertile in Java.

Until a few decades ago the archipelago provided its inhabitants with an abundant food supply. This is no longer true. Rapid population growth, food shortages, and the need to import large quantities of foodstuffs to prevent starvation characterize the postwar period, and particularly the past ten years.

Sharply expanded cultivation and the growing of cash crops under pressure from the colonial rulers enabled the population to multiply more than five times in the nineteenth century and three times in the first half of the twentieth. Even as the enlarged food base and general economic advance in that 150-year period seem to have propelled the birthrate, simultaneous developments cut down sharply on death rates. As the Dutch extended their police control to end the perpetual warfare among principalities and tribes, and as they introduced public health measures to suppress infectious and other diseases and reduce infant deaths, population growth started to become a problem.

Thus when economic progress slowed down in the 1950's and then ground to a standstill, the task of feeding Indonesia's growing population assumed crisis proportions.

Overall, Indonesia's population density is twice that of the United States: the country accommodates on 744,000 square miles (one-fourth the area of the continental United States) an estimated 110 million people, or slightly more than half the population of the United States. However, such averages are somewhat deceptive. Java, the most populous island, now contains about 70 million people in an area barely one-third the size of California. Java's population density is now 1,200 people per square mile—20 times the density rate of the United States. Governmental efforts to resettle large numbers of Javanese on the outer islands have not been very successful.

Indonesia's current population growth rate, at 2.2% per year, is twice the U.S. rate of 1.1%, but not especially high when compared with Thailand's 3.0%, Malaysia's 3.1%, or the Philippines' 3.3%. Nevertheless, the residents of those other countries have been improving their living standards, while Indonesians have less to eat today than before the war because productivity has not kept pace with population growth. Not only have the agricultural methods of the small farmers improved very little since the time, about 200 years ago, when Java's population totalled a mere three million (or since the turn of the twentieth century when it approximated 20 million, compared with the present 70 million), but the efficiency of estate operations in the production of such commercial crops as rubber, sugar, tea, coffee, tobacco, and copra has sharply fallen, particularly in the past ten years.

In a country in which agriculture accounts for 70% of the employment, for more than one-half the national income, and for almost two-thirds of all exports, agricultural decline cannot easily be offset even by significant advances in industry and commerce. As we shall see later, some of Indonesia's major industries and trade activities have contracted in recent years. Indonesian economic statistics are both inaccurate and unreliable, but it appears probable that Indonesia is one of the few countries in which per-capita income has actually declined since prewar days. In a country in which at least 85% of the people live at a bare subsistence level, a further reduction, no matter how small, inevitably causes widespread and intense suffering, of which there is much evidence.

Most of Indonesia's people appear industrious to the extent necessary to secure a livelihood, but they do not, on the whole, display a driving ambition for economic advancement. The great majority of inhabitants are of Malay stock and belong to the same major ethnic family as the indigenous population of the Malay Peninsula. They also adhere, more or less, to the Muslim faith. Only after 1824, when the British and the Dutch divided the area among themselves, assigning the Malay Peninsula to the former and the archipelago to the latter, did differences appear and gradually widen between the indigenous majorities of the two areas in language, customs, and attitudes. These differences were due, at least in part, to differing colonial policies of the British and Netherlands governments. Malays and Indonesians regard each other as brothers and, now that the 1963-65 "confrontation" has come to an end, are starting to act again, if not as brothers, at least as good neighbors.

Indonesia's Chinese population is proportionally far smaller than Malaysia's—a mere 3% compared with Malaysia's 36%. But just as in Malaysia and elsewhere, the clear division of economic functions by ethnic group seems more than a historical accident. The hard-driving Chinese dominate—or used to dominate prior to the severe restrictions imposed on them within the past ten years—the small and medium-scale commerce; they were the merchants and the bankers. They gathered and bought products from the farmers and craftsmen, sold manufactured and imported goods to them, and lent them money. If carried on by an ethnically or religiously distinct minority, these activities have traditionally elicited from the indigenous majority, economically less active and less successful, a dislike and then a hatred which in many lands has developed into repression and erupted as persecution.

This is true in Indonesia, and has led to a net emigration of the Chinese in recent years. If political conditions in potentially recipient countries were not extremely unfavorable, such emigration might be much greater. In the aftermath of the attempted communist *coup d'état* in September 1965, between 250,000 and 500,000 people, many of them Chinese, were killed, according to several estimates (no reliable figures are known and no adequate details are available as of now). That this encouraged many of the remaining Chinese to grab any opportunity, however uncertain or unappealing, to leave Indonesia, is understandable. On the whole, the Chinese never played as important a role in Indonesia as they did and still do in Malaysia. This may offer a partial explanation for the difference in the public policies which the two countries followed in colonial times and for the even more divergent policies pursued by them since independence.

There were absolutely and proportionately more Europeans in Indonesia than in Malaysia during colonial times and in the first few years of independence. This was so largely because the small size of the resident Chinese population caused the Dutch to import more of their own nationals to fill the jobs.[3] In 1958-60, however, the Dutch were expelled, and many other foreigners left soon after; according to recent estimates, only about 6,000 Europeans and Americans now live in Indonesia.[4]

In Java and on some of the other major islands, Indonesia enjoys a greater ethnic homogeneity of the population than Malaysia. This eases or eliminates some of the political and other problems with which Malaysia has to wrestle and which cause uncertainty in regard to its internal peaceful development. But the greater homogeneity does not seem to have helped to propel Indonesia toward more rapid social and economic development. Quite the contrary. An essential element seems to be lacking, and the efforts of the Indonesian government toward accelerated progress have failed.

[3] See preceding chapter footnotes 12 and 13.
[4] Since 1966 the number of Westerners in Indonesia has been increasing.

Indonesia's economy, as mentioned before, is largely a subsistence economy. The farmer, it has been said, is happy if he can grow enough food for himself and his family and can get 30 feet of textile a year—as he could prior to World War II. Of late, however, too many farmers cannot produce sufficient crops to feed their larger families from ever-smaller—because further divided—plots. Textiles are scarce because sufficient foreign currency is lacking to import enough cotton, which cannot be grown locally.

By far the most important food crop is rice, supplemented by maize, cassava roots, sweet potatoes, and soybeans. Rice used to be abundant in Java and the other islands, but between 1960 and 1965 the government, threatened by widespread famine, had to import an average of 761,000 tons of rice annually at a cost of about $100 million. To the extent to which the cost exceeded specially authorized grants and loans, it depleted the country's foreign exchange holdings, so desperately needed to pay for manufactured products, raw materials, and the spare parts to keep machinery in operation. In 1964 and 1965 when exports and foreign exchange earnings fell low, the government found it impossible to purchase sufficient rice abroad. With U.S. aid then unavailable, the price of rice soared and starvation was reported in many areas.

Rice and other basic food crops are grown mostly in smallholdings averaging about two acres in area. Irrigation is widely practiced because rice, except the dry variety, consumes huge amounts of water. The areas under irrigation were rapidly expanded during colonial times, particularly in the decades just prior to World War II, but not much has been added since. Huge expansion schemes were drawn—on paper —but actual construction and maintenance were barely sufficient to keep the existing irrigation system going. Fertilizer and farm machinery are little used. The average rice yield per acre increased on Indonesian paddies by 10% between

the years 1950-54 and 1960-64, but on Malaysian paddies by
19%. Yield per hectare equalled, in the average of 1960-64: in
Indonesia 1790 kg, in Malaysia 2090 kg, in Taiwan 3220 kg,
in Japan 5040 kg.

Farming in Indonesia is supplemented by fishing in the
waters surrounding the islands and in rivers and lakes, but the
methods are primitive and the catch modest. Livestock
(mostly cattle) is widely grown, but is used largely for plow-
ing and for pulling carts. As long as crops are in short supply
and pasture or rangeland is at a premium, animals will not be
grown for their meat or dairy products. There are simply more
calories in crops when eaten directly by humans than in those
"processed" through livestock. This in turn means that little
animal fertilizer is available and that the human diet is often
unbalanced.

Indonesia's commercial crops are grown largely on the
outer islands, mostly on estates which, prior to government
seizure, were foreign-owned. Almost none of those crops,
with the exception of the spices for which the islands have
long been famous, are indigenous. Dutch planters gradually
introduced rubber, sugar, coffee, tea, tobacco, copra, oil palm,
and many other crops as a result of long, costly experiments
by trial and error. Over long periods the Dutch East Indies
ranked among the world's leading suppliers of those and other
tropical products which earned much of the country's foreign
exchange.

The plantation system suffered a heavy blow when the
Dutch owners and managers were interned by the Japanese
during World War II. The system never recovered; the new
government after the war frowned on the possession of
estates by non-Indonesians, so that many of the Dutch farmers
did not resume their former operations. The expulsion of the
Dutch in 1958-60 ended the plantation system, and the government took over most of the estates still active—about one-

fourth of the original estate acreage. Many of those estates are now idle, and are being gradually swallowed up by forests and jungles. Others are inadequately and wastefully run by government-appointed managers. The sharp drop in acreage and production of most commercial crops to below prewar levels has, of course, caused a heavy loss in foreign exchange earnings.

Some Indonesian farmers began to grow rubber trees, but there was no development comparable to that of Malaysia in replacement of old trees or replanting with high-yield varieties. Ambitious plans were drawn for the rejuvenation of rubber trees, but they were never carried out. In fact, because there has been little research and technical advance, today more than half of the rubber acreage is planted with trees that are over-age or nearly so. Indonesia, once the world's largest producer of natural rubber, yielded first position to Malaysia in the late 1950's and has been sliding down farther ever since. Runaway inflation and government-established low prices have discouraged production but have stimulated smuggling.

The history of most other commercial and export crops in the past 20 years, and particularly in the past ten, parallels the sad story of rubber: with few exceptions, Indonesia's output has shrunk either absolutely or relatively, in comparison to the production records of other Asiatic countries.

Nor has Indonesia done better in the extraction of the minerals with which it is richly endowed. It used to be the world's second biggest supplier of tin, but output has now fallen to less than half of the 1954 total. Production of coal, iron, salt, iodine, and other minerals has likewise declined as the government has declared all mineral deposits to be national property and has taken them over.

Only in the production of crude petroleum and natural gas, in which Indonesia, with its Sumatra fields, leads Asia east of

Iran, has there been a significant improvement. Here production has increased almost 50% since the late 1950's. It should be noted, however, that Iran has more than doubled its output during the same time span. Until recently, Indonesian petroleum production was largely in private hands. To be sure, petroleum exploration and operations were declared to be state functions, along with other activities in the extractive industries. But for technological and export reasons as well as because of the necessity of selling most of the output abroad (and because Iran's experience with the nationalization of oil was well remembered) the government let the three major companies and some smaller firms continue in operation. However, it placed them under increasing pressure. The Shell Oil Company decided in 1965 to sell out to the government, to be paid off mostly in a share of future crude oil production. Stanvac continued operations as best it could but Caltex (a joint venture of the Standard Oil Company of California and Texaco, Inc.) expanded and was able, despite heavy obstacles, to enlarge its output substantially.

The bulk of Indonesia's mineral wealth as well as much of its estate (export crop) operations, and thus the main sources of foreign exchange earnings, are located on the outer islands —Sumatra, Borneo (Kalimantan), Celebes (Sulawesi). Political, civic, religious, and tribal leaders on those islands have come to feel increasingly that overpopulated Java constitutes a drain on their resources, and that they are being exploited and ruled by the Javanese far more onerously than they ever were by the Dutch. That their rulers are brown rather than white does not pacify them. Unanswered grievances sparked an open revolt in 1957-58, which President Sukarno suppressed with a show of overwhelming military superiority. However, the upheaval and its aftermath did not, of course, further economic improvement in the islands or in Java.

In Indonesia, as in most "developing" countries, manufacturing focuses largely on the processing of local products, crops, and minerals. Such consumer goods as foodstuffs, tobacco, metals, and wood are being made from local raw materials. Some Indonesian countries, however, depend largely or wholly on the importation of raw materials. The textile industry is large but almost no cotton (and very little wool) is produced in the islands. Synthetics could be manufactured from local petroleum products, but no such operation has been started or envisioned; the capital investment and managerial and technical skills required are not now available. It is the scarcity of these items—investment capital and managerial and technical talent—that restricts more rapid industrial expansion of any kind, although governmental multi-year plans in Indonesia, as in many similarly situated countries, have placed heavy emphasis upon such expansion. There is little local saving, and little incentive under prevailing public policies to invest savings productively.

Since the declared goal of the postwar governments has been a socialistic state with public ownership of most means of production, foreign capitalists have had little incentive to risk their money on questionable ventures in Indonesia. The Indonesian government invited foreign investment, but also did its level best to discourage it from coming. Steadily expanding nationalization of private industry without adequate —or any—compensation, and the repression of the remaining private enterprises gave clear warning to foreign capital to stay out.

Developed in colonial times, Indonesia's major industries were largely owned and managed by foreigners; of these, most were Dutch, and some British, American, German, or Belgian. In the 1950's and early 1960's, these industries were either expropriated by the government or placed under strict government control. Medium-sized and small industries had been founded and operated largely by Chinese, who often acted as middlemen. Recently the government has increasingly restricted the economic activities of the Chinese population, either by outright prohibition of commercial ownership or operations or by steadily mounting indirect pressures. As has been discovered, it was easier to drive the Chinese out of business than to replace them with Indonesians who could operate their trades as efficiently and successfully. The net loss was to both the Chinese and the Indonesians, and to their economy.

When the Indonesian government found that foreign investors and entrepreneurs were deterred by its policies and actions and were unwilling to provide the huge sums demanded or needed, it pinned its hopes to the receipt of aid from foreign governments. Playing off one side against the other, Sukarno managed to get more than $800 million from the U.S. government in the postwar period, and a like amount from the U.S.S.R., for economic purposes, aside from $1 billion in military aid from the Soviets and sizeable sums from other Western and Eastern nations, either as grants or as loans, many of which—as should have been apparent—Indonesia probably will never be able to redeem.

No overall index of industrial production, such as those published by most countries, is available for Indonesia. But it is evident to knowledgeable observers that despite the flamboyant announcements and sporadic actions subsequent to independence, Indonesia is in industrial progress far behind comparable countries. A sizeable share of the existing plant is not operating, either for lack of spare parts (due to scarcity or misapplication of foreign exchange), inadequate maintenance, incompetent management, or absence of sufficient capital and raw materials.

Indonesia's overseas trade has shrunk in the past 12 years, as it was bound to do when the production of export crops and most minerals except petroleum declined. The resulting scarcity of foreign exchange has cut the import potential. Moreover, most trading and shipping concerns, which had been in Dutch hands, collapsed when the Dutch were expelled. The remaining firms reduced operations sharply when the Indonesian government took them over. Trade relations with greater Southeast Asia's commercial and financial center, Singapore, were ruptured by Indonesia at the start of its "Crush Malaysia" campaign. That break was, of course, like cutting off one's nose to spite one's face. In this case, as in many of its general policies, the Indonesian government followed an emotional rather than a rational line and subordinated economic to political considerations. Indonesia's people have been paying—and continue to pay—a heavy price for letting their first postwar government continue in power so long.

A comparison of the economic history of Indonesia with that of Malaysia in the postwar period shows two significant differences, which undoubtedly are related to their differing fortunes:

1) Indonesia followed a socialistic policy of government ownership and control of the means of production, while Malaysia pursued a free-enterprise policy.

2) Indonesia expelled the Dutch managers and technicians and suppressed the small number of Chinese merchants and craftsmen. Malaysia, on the other hand, took no action against resident Europeans or Americans and left its large Chinese population free to expand in the fields of commerce, industry, trade, and finance which all, in consequence, developed rapidly. Indonesia's population now includes at most 3% Chinese and six Westerners per 100,000 residents. Malaysia has a 36% Chinese population and 200 Westerners for every 100,000 residents.

The presence or absence of Westerners and Chinese is no mere accident, but the result of public policy related to economic philosophy and racial restriction.

To gain a better perspective on developments in Indonesia it will be helpful to follow its history from colonial times to the present. This may give us a keener insight into the dynamic forces that shaped its fortunes.

FROM COLONY TO INDEPENDENCE

The islands which now comprise the Republic of Indonesia were governed for thousands of years by numerous steadily warring local rulers, who in turn were sporadically conquered by other invaders. In the seventeenth century, the Dutch started to form in this area the colonial empire which they controlled for almost 300 years. At the outset, they had no intention toward territorial aggrandizement. They were attracted, like the Portuguese, Spanish, and British, by the prospect of profitable trade with the fabulous "spice islands," and they founded the Netherlands East India Company to ply trade in pepper and other spices. Like other European powers, they soon learned that, to protect their safety and property and to assure the fulfillment of contracts, they had to assume political and military control. They did so reluctantly, because of the exorbitant costs which indeed consumed most of their profits. By the end of the eighteenth century, the Dutch East India Company was bankrupt and the Netherlands government had to take it over and establish a colony. This greatly boosted Holland's prestige and position in the world, but the colony turned out to be something less than a rousing financial success. The British so learned when they assumed control of it during the years of Napoleonic rule in Europe. As a result, they returned the colony to the Netherlands government soon after Waterloo.

For most of the ensuing century and a half of colonial rule, the Dutch tried a system of *laissez faire*—free and unrestricted enterprise. They soon found that the Indonesians were not responding to traditional economic incentives and would not voluntarily grow export crops such as sugar, indigo, coffee, tea, and tobacco.

In the 1830's the Dutch imposed the *cultuurstelsel,* usually translated as *culture system,* but actually a cultivation system for agricultural products to assure through indirect means the growing and production of export crops. In all other economic activities, free enterprise was maintained. This system motivated Dutchmen as well as Chinese residents of the islands to engage in entrepreneurship in a wide variety of fields, on plantations, in manufacturing, in commerce, and in shipping. The profit incentive, as before, proved ineffective in regard to the great majority of the indigenous population, which was steadily losing ground to foreigners. Late in the nineteenth century the government therefore adopted what it called the "ethical policy," a dual standard which offered advantages and gave protection to native Indonesians, who apparently would not, or possibly could not compete with Europeans and Chinese in an open market.

The *theory* of the double standard is highly controversial and today generally discredited. Even references to it are resented. But the *practice* of discrimination in favor of economically less effective groups, ethnic or other, has become standard policy throughout the world and is today hardly questioned. The general trend seems to be in the direction of weighting the scales more heavily against the economically successful by using multiple standards.

That government intervened more directly and forcefully in the economy in the Dutch East Indies than it did on the Malay Peninsula may not be due to a greater predilection for governmental action on the part of the Dutch than of the British authorities. It is more likely that the economic incentives of a free market provided sufficient motivation in Malaya because of the presence after 1870 of a large group, the Chinese, who were more ready and willing to rise to the challenge than the indigenous population. In the islands the number of persons with the economic drive to respond to such incentives was more limited, so that a government anxious to accelerate development felt impelled to proceed to direct action.

This hypothesis of the interrelationship of economic policy and population characteristics offers a possible explanation of the different nature of policy in Malaysia and Indonesia and the striking difference in their economic fortunes. As of now, it is no more than a hypothesis—but one which needs to be studied in connection with developmental efforts in many countries and eventually either confirmed or discarded. It cannot now be advanced as a firm and proven conclusion.

The Japanese occupation during World War II ended Dutch rule in the East Indies. When Japan surrendered in 1945, Sukarno and his followers organized a revolution against the reestablished colonial regime. They were militarily not very successful, but they continued to fight on for four years in the expectation, justified as it proved, that growing pressure on the Netherlands government by the United States and other countries to relinquish its possessions in the Pacific area would eventually become irresistible.

At the close of 1949 the Netherlands government granted independence to the United States of Indonesia, a parliamentary democracy with a federal structure which assumed numerous obligations to guarantee individual and regional rights, few of which were carried out and many of which were later unilaterally renounced. The federal system was discarded within a few months and other democratic safeguards fell one by one, though the 1949-50 constitution lingered on for ten years until it was abolished by presidential decree. The Indonesian people had greeted the end of the long and often harsh and heavy-handed Dutch colonial rule and the establishment of their independence as a nation with enthusiasm, and had given it wholehearted and overwhelming support. As it turned out, the mass of people had little more control over their government and its policies after independence than before. From its inception, the Indonesian republic was under an ever-tightening one-man rule limited only by its own ability to carry out what it planned and to enforce what it decreed.

When the Netherlands government yielded to the inevitable and withdrew from the islands, there was in Indonesia a common belief, shared by much of the rest of the world, that *merdeka* (independence) would automatically bring in its wake prosperity for everyone. Indonesia's people, and the peoples of many other lands, had been told time and again by their revolutionary leaders that only the wicked imperialists, the colonial exploiters, were holding them back, were depriving them of the fruits of their labor and of the natural resources that were rightfully theirs, and that greedy capitalists were preventing them from having a life of plenty. All that was necessary, so the story went, was for the people to get their hands on the huge profits which the colonial masters were expropriating from the suppressed workers.

Sukarno and his followers were no less certain that Indonesia would thenceforth prosper than they were that the Netherlands faced economic hardship or ruin. Holland, a small country with then only 11 million inhabitants and one of the world's highest population density rates (934 per square mile), but almost no natural resources, was being divorced from its major possession, a resource-rich island chain with 100 million people who had been slaving to amass wealth for their colonial masters. From now on Holland's economic fortunes would surely be reversed. Little did Sukarno, or anyone else for that matter, think in 1949 that, after 17 years of his unrestricted rule, Indonesia would be so impoverished and Holland so well off that the Indonesian Minister for Finance and Economic Affairs would have to travel to The Hague, hat in hand, to plead for aid and to offer compensation for past expropriations.

Nor did any of the revolutionary leaders at the time think, or at least dare to say, that the people's prospect for a better life depended on their willingness to work harder and more efficiently than before, and to make sacrifices from current consumption so as to permit the capital accumulation and technological progress without which it would be impossible to raise productivity and living standards.[5]

The Netherlands, relieved of what in retrospect seems to have been "white man's burden" more than "colonialist exploitation," experienced a period of unprecedented economic growth in the 15 succeeding years. Its gross product and income more than doubled in *constant prices* and grew 60% on a per-capita basis. Exports more than tripled in constant

[5] Barbara Ward explained this apparently naive outlook when she said that emphasis on work effort, austerity, and saving is unknown outside the western world and that self-discipline and self-denial are known in the eastern world only *without* work (Barbara Ward, *The Rich Nations and the Poor Nations*, New York, W. W. Norton & Co., 1962, p. 38). Later on (pp. 87-99), she explains that "it is a simple fact of human nature that you do not get what you do not want, and you do not work for what you can't imagine. . . ." and ". . . that some societies still lack this drive toward material advance and change." While Miss Ward uses mainly examples from African experience, similar observations can be made in Asiatic countries. Whether the reference to "some societies" implies an ethnic basis is unclear. But it is evident that the political leaders of some countries which "lack this drive toward material advance and change" nevertheless expect and demand advance and change not by efforts of their own people but by efforts of the nations that are prosperous by virtue of their having exerted such efforts for several centuries. Miss Ward feels that countries which lack the drive are entitled to support from the countries which have it. That proposition is now widely but not universally accepted.

prices, gold holdings more than quintupled, the value of its currency remained steady, and unemployment equalled less than 1% of the labor force. Holland's financial and economic situation was as stable and secure as before the "loss" of Indonesia, if not more so.

Indonesia designed ambitious multi-year plans which failed abysmally, while Holland more than fulfilled its "indicative" plans, which were not really comprehensive economic plans but merely projections to serve as guides, prepared with the cooperation of the business community. Indonesia steadily tightened its control over the economic life, sought to halt the slide by confiscating first the vast holdings of the Dutch and then those of other foreign nationals, and finally, when all else failed, engaged in foreign military adventures to divert the people's attention from their misery.

In a speech on June 1, 1945, demanding independence, Sukarno first announced the five principles (*Pantjasila*) which have been regarded as Indonesia's goals and guidelines ever since: (1) Nationalism, (2) Internationalism, (3) Democracy, (4) Social Justice, (5) Belief in God. The sequence was later modified, but *Pantjasila* is still upheld, even though Sukarno is no longer in office. Eighteen years after announcing *Pantjasila*, in his Independence Day speech on August 17, 1963, he had to admit that he had failed to deliver on his promises, and he asked the people for patience "just a little while longer." However, their patience had by then almost run out, and Sukarno fell from power a little more than two years later.

One of Sukarno's earliest companions, Mohammad Hatta, who had been a leader in the nationalist movement since 1922—longer than Sukarno himself—and who served as vice president and then as prime minister during the fight for independence between 1945 and 1949, admitted in the summer of 1966 that Indonesians were then worse off than under the

Dutch, "when minimum wages could as least buy five kilo-grams of rice per day." [6]

How did all this come about? Why did Indonesia, the sixth largest nation on earth in terms of population, and a country endowed with abundant natural resources, suffer such mis-fortunes that after 16 years of independence it was bankrupt and in a state of crisis, its people suffering and barely able to get enough food—despite having received generous foreign aid from both sides of the Iron Curtain?

The more closely we study the history of the postwar years, the more persuasive the proposition becomes that the policies which the government pursued bear a major responsibility for the downward slide. Virtually all of the revolutionary leaders who joined the new government in one capacity or another had a strong socialist background. This is not sur-prising. It is understandable that "have-nots" resent the "haves," that they blame the social and economic system for the difference in their respective fortunes, and that they strongly feel the need for discarding a system that made others, most of them foreigners, rich and kept themselves and their brothers poor.

"Every educated Asian," said Indonesia's first Prime Minis-ter Sutan Sjharir in 1953, "living in an underdeveloped coun-try and dreaming of the possibility of his country's achieving real and factual equality with the rich and modern West, must ultimately resort to Socialistic thinking." [7] The example of the U.S.S.R. suggested to many that socialism could transform a

[6] *Far Eastern Economic Review,* June 16, 1966, p. 519.

[7] *Far Eastern Economic Review,* August 4, 1966, p. 179. Mr. Sjharir did not mention that the Asiatic countries which are economically progressing and have good reason to dream of achieving real and factual equality with the rich and modern West are following free enterprise policies, while many examples suggest that most countries which pursue socialistic goals will long be restricted to dreaming without coming much closer to the fulfillment of their dreams.

backward country more quickly into an industrialized and powerful nation than could the kind of slow and painful industrial revolution under capitalist auspices that took place in Western countries somewhat earlier. Soviet claims about equality in the "classless society," the absence of exploitation, and the inevitability of eventual socialist triumph over the capitalist countries naturally appealed to those who had the psychological need to blame their poverty on the "system" rather than on more substantial factors which were much harder to correct, if they could be corrected at all.[8]

To the young Indonesians who hated the colonial regime, socialism and nationalism became simply the two sides of the banner under which the students of the 1920's and 1930's fought in the movements that produced most of the political leaders of the revolution and postwar government.[9] All parties in the new republic subscribed to socialism of one kind or another; none favored private enterprise or free markets. Their pronouncements made it amply clear that they were anxious to abolish private ownership and replace it with a state-operated structure: an economy ruled by intelligence and planned to provide social justice and prosperity for all seemed greatly preferable to allowing the jungle of market competition and private profit to continue to inflict suffering on millions of humble people.

Virtually all large-scale enterprise was at that time in Western hands, and most middle-sized undertakings were controlled by the Chinese. Determined though the new gov-

[8] One of the few Indonesian scholars able to see the causal relationships clearly is S. Takdir Alisjahbana, who in *Indonesia: Cultural and Social Revolution* (Singapore, Oxford University Press, 1966) attributes the indigence of the Indonesian people to elements within their own social framework rather than to the bogey of colonialism and imperialism.

[9] The communists often foment upheaval and revolution in colonial or formerly colonial lands by stirring up or assisting in what they call a "war of national liberation." This hitches two strong emotions to their chariot and mobilizes support which the red banner alone could not muster.

ernment was to free the country of foreign capitalist domination, it recognized that Indonesians were not yet ready to take
over. There were few Indonesians who possessed the necessary competence to move into technical, professional, and
managerial jobs. Experience under the Dutch regime had
shown that there were even fewer with the ambition and
drive to accept the challenge as entrepreneurs. Thus the
despised capitalism had to be endured as a stepping stone to
the socialist society, but only until a sufficient number of Indonesians had been trained to assume responsibility and command as the technicians and managers of the new order.

FROM INDEPENDENCE TO RUIN

In the treaty granting Indonesia independence, the new
country agreed to assume certain obligations, such as the
establishment of a federal system to safeguard the liberty and
interests of the residents of the outer islands against Javanese
domination, guarantees for the personal and property rights
of the Dutch and other foreign nationals, fair compensation in
case of nationalization of enterprises or property, responsibility for the Netherlands Indies' public debt, and the guarantee of consultation on major financial decisions. However,
most of these agreements were unilaterally renounced by the
Indonesian government, some within a few months, others in
a few years.

In the first few years of independence Indonesia's people
and their leaders saw the future in the brightest terms, now
that the higher political, military, and administrative positions
so long denied them were available. Only one cloud cast a
shadow on the universal bliss: though Indonesians immediately took over the political command posts, they could not as
easily move into the management of economic affairs. Virtu-

ally all plantations and large enterprises in mineral extraction and other industries, commerce, finance, and shipping, had been founded by foreigners—mostly Dutch, some British or American—and were managed by them and wholly dependent on foreign capital and skill. Only a few Indonesian nationals had the competence to assume the managerial and technical positions—and most of these were of Chinese descent. Outright nationalization or confiscation would have created chaos; therefore, the new leaders had to bridle their impatience and defer plans to "Indonesianize" the modern sector of the economy. But they were firmly determined that this was not a change in the direction in which they meant to travel and only a matter of the time table. Public declarations, however, left no doubt about the intention to eliminate foreigners from the Indonesian economy as rapidly as possible. Since all governmental leaders were dedicated socialists, it was clear that Indonesianization meant appropriation by the government. Besides, they knew that not many Indonesians had given evidence of possessing an entrepreneurial spirit, and that it was at least doubtful that even if given the chance, they would be able to replace foreign owners and managers within a few years.

Westerners in the large companies did not have to read the handwriting on the wall: they were told in no uncertain terms that they would be tolerated and permitted to operate a little longer, but that their time was running out. Many understood this and shaped their plans accordingly. Most Westerners, however, were so convinced of their own irreplaceability, and of the improbability that native Indonesians could, even in decades, develop a management and professional class competent to take over their firms and direct intricate industrial and commercial operations that they expected to be around—and in the saddle—for a long time to come. They thought that for reasons of self-interest, after weighing the realities of the situation and making decisions by logic rather than emotion, a rational Indonesian government would cooperate with them to prevent economic suicide. They believed, in sum, that the Indonesian government would act as they would have under similar circumstances. In this belief they could not have been more mistaken. President Sukarno and his associates regarded economic policy as a tool of political strategy, as a reflection of Indonesian social and cultural aims. They viewed the economy as a servant which had to carry out commands from above and not "talk back." And in this view, the Indonesian leaders in turn were badly mistaken. Like a human being or an animal, an economy responds well to kind treatment, but it can pack a powerful wallop when its needs are ignored or its rules of existence violated. It "kicks back" or it languishes.

Indonesia's government had, at the time of independence, some justification for believing its policies would help achieve its goals. The majority of economists then active in development work favored centralized planning and strong governmental action as an effective means of rapidly propelling backward countries to higher levels. Many of them have since learned a lesson from a solid record of failures. Two recent works on the subject illustrate this lesson well. The main theme of a recent symposium volume based on extensive World Bank experience, *Development Planning: Lessons of Experience*,[10] is that governments of most low-income countries today are not yet ready to carry out comprehensive development planning, and that they do not now have the technical, administrative, and political competence to assume command of the major economic activities of their citizens.

In a Brookings Institution volume entitled *Economic Policies Toward Less Developed Countries* (1967), Harry G.

[10] Albert Waterston, with C. J. Martin, A. T. Schumacher, and F. A. Steuber, *Development Planning: Lessons of Experience*, Baltimore, Johns Hopkins Press, 1965.

Johnson of the London School of Economics relates disappointing performance of the poorer countries to their own policies as well as to the trade and aid policies of the industrial nations, but he places the main blame on the policies of the less developed countries themselves:

> Their nationalistic orientation to economic policy, their preference for centralized economic planning, their exploitative attitude toward traditional agriculture, their commitment to import substitution, their policies of inflation and currency overvaluation, and their hostility to private investment in their industry by foreigners can all be adduced in explanation of their export problems.

The government of the Republic of Indonesia not only made it clear at the outset that it intended to reduce and eventually eliminate foreign management; it proceeded forthwith to discriminate against non-Indonesian firms. It used all means at its command to make life unpleasant and unprofitable for those companies and their personnel and to subject them to harassment. This did not cause many major corporations with heavy investment to pull out immediately at a heavy loss. Few corporations, however, were willing to commit further funds even for modernization or reparation of immense war damages, let alone for further expansion. Many, in fact, prepared for a gradual contraction and, later, as the government became increasingly hostile, for eventual liquidation. Western companies long engaged in overseas ventures are usually willing to incur substantial calculated commercial risks if the profit potential is commensurate. However, when the political risks become too high and profit potentials are deliberately cut or eliminated, they tend to seek greener pastures.

An investment retrenchment in a country with vast and

urgent capital needs cannot but gravely affect its economic development. The reluctance of private investors did not cause Indonesian government leaders to ease their attitude; in fact, it was strengthened. The fact that private capital was not forthcoming only proved to Indonesian leaders that more extensive public action was needed. The favored alternative to private investment was aid from foreign governments. The United States obligingly provided between 1945 and 1963, more than $800 million. When tax revenues and aid became inadequate to meet ambitious development plans, Indonesia's government resorted to deficit financing through the operation of the banknote printing press. This brought rapid inflation, which caused wage demands and project costs to rise. Official exchange rates were kept below free-market rates, which encouraged imports and discouraged exports. The inflationary spiral, once started, kept accelerating. Finally it became uncontrollable.

In 1951 the government budget was still almost balanced, but in each of the succeeding six years expenditures exceeded revenues (including foreign aid, loans, etc.) by 15 to 25%. In 1958 and 1959 public outlays were 50% greater than income; in 1962 and 1963 they were twice as large; in 1964 and 1965 they were about two and a half times as great; and in 1966 they were more than three times as large. Rapid currency expansion resulted as deficits were covered by advances from the Bank of Indonesia. Total money supply climbed from 4.4 billion rupiahs in 1950 to 11 billion in 1954, to 19 billion in 1957, to 48 billion in 1960, to 265 billion in 1963, to 2,714 billion in 1964, and to 28,000 billion in early 1967.[11]

Consumers' prices doubled between 1950 and 1954, more

[11] All figures in "old" rupiahs. Indonesian economic and financial statistics are not always consistent or comparable. While numerous tables have been published, they often disagree with one another or differ as to earlier year data. The data given here are from official publications and attempt to give as consistent a picture as possible.

than doubled between 1954 and 1958, more than doubled again between 1958 and 1961. From 1961 to 1964 prices multiplied fourteen times, from 1964 to 1965 again seven times, and in the succeeding year more than eight times. Since the inception of the republic, prices have multiplied about 10,000 times. Though history has recorded several cases of more extreme inflation—particularly in Europe after World War I —it is easy to see that such hyperinflation wreaks havoc on the economy, the living standards, and the confidence and morale of the great mass of the people. As elsewhere, inflation led in Indonesia to recurring unrest among the workers, breakdown of discipline, and almost universal impoverishment and misery. However, once a government has come to rely on the printing press as the solution to economic and financial problems, it is extremely difficult, if not politically impossible, to reverse the trend, even if the cause of inflation is acknowledged and condemned. Inflation, like narcotic drugs, is sometimes resorted to as a convenient but presumably temporary means of resolving pressing problems. It is habit-forming, however, and can become irresistible even as it runs its course of destruction.

Indonesia's economic difficulties did not end here. When rapid inflation is accompanied by tight government control of most economic activities—and the resulting underpayment of public employees—widespread corruption is the usual result.

The Dutch had maintained a sometimes harsh but honest and reasonably efficient regime. In contrast, the main characteristics of the republican administration were corruption, bribery, and incompetence—at all levels. Whoever needed something from the government—a license, a permit, correction of a grievance, an order for goods or services—had to fulfill the wishes of the officials in power—without presenting a bill if he were wise. In addition, labor costs were rising, but production was falling and the paperwork and time required to import needed machines, raw materials, and spare parts grew immensely.

An increasing number of foreign plantation owners and merchants gave up the struggle and abandoned valuable holdings that had been built up over many decades. Often local indigenous workers took over such holdings and demanded that the government continue to keep them in operation by meeting their deficits—and the government obliged.

By the mid-1950's, it became obvious to all concerned that the expected economic growth was not being achieved, that the prosperity which was to follow independence was as far away as ever, and that financial and economic troubles were multiplying. ECAFE tried to soften its 1955 report by saying that "during 1954-55 the economy of Indonesia was still in a transitional stage" and ". . . the economy was not stabilized."

Several attempts were then made at remedial action. The National Planning Board (*Bappenas*) drew up an ambitious five-year plan for 1956-60, elections for a parliament were held, and appeals were made for more substantial foreign aid. However, the five-year plan of development by government was soon in trouble and fell far short of its goals. Steps to establish parliamentary democracy were soon abandoned.

On May 17, 1956, President Sukarno addressed a joint session of the U. S. Congress and pleaded not only for large-scale aid ("America is known the world over for generosity . . .") but also for aid without strings, to be used at the discretion of the Indonesian government ("For the furtherance of their functions as defenders of freedom, America and Indonesia need to realize how to obtain lasting results, and these depend upon the specific conditions of Asian countries and the development of the national aspirations of the Asian people, which indeed, America cannot be expected immediately to know or to understand").

President Sukarno emphasized that the Indonesian people could not be expected to finance their aspirations, as the Western nations had done, but looked to the West for the necessary capital: "There is no imposition upon the people [of Indonesia] to save part of their meager income as a means of accumulating badly needed capital, neither would we introduce forced labor for national undertakings, nor the expropriation of existing big companies which are run mainly on the basis of profit motives."

Nevertheless, within slightly over a year after that plea, the Indonesian government proceeded to expropriate all Dutch property on the islands—plantations and industrial, commercial, mining and residential holdings accumulated over generations and worth billions of dollars. The government also renounced its foreign debts and discontinued retirement pay to former Dutch East Indies government employees. These actions were declared to be in retaliation for the unwillingness of the Netherlands government to hand over West New Guinea.

A few years later, British support for Malaysia against invasion by Indonesian armed forces served as justification for taking over most British properties, just as American imperialism and hostility (discontinuation of financial aid to Indonesia) were cited as reasons for taking similar action in regard to most American holdings, which totalled about half a billion dollars. Further, when unilateral abrogation or disregard of solemn treaty obligations brought forth mere paper protests but no effective remedial or retaliatory action on the part of the Western powers, Indonesia and some other countries were encouraged in continuing on their path, just as in the 1930's Western failure to punish flagrant violations of the peace treaties by Germany led to ever more drastic aggression.

It appears quite likely, for example, that the outcome of

the Suez Canal affair in 1956-57 influenced Indonesian attitudes and actions in regard to West New Guinea and against
the property and persons of Dutch citizenship, and subsequently against other Western nationals.

West New Guinea (Irian Barat) is populated by primitive
tribes which are not related to Indonesians by descent, language, or customs. But it had been part of the Netherlands
East Indies—the only part that was not turned over to the new
republic in 1949-50—and became a symbol: "the last territorial demand." The demand was largely irrational. West New
Guinea was a heavy economic liability to the Dutch, as it
later proved to be to the Indonesians. The Dutch resisted
transfer because this was the last vestige of their Eastern
empire—and because they felt that the issue should be
decided *by* the New Guineans (by election, as agreed in the
1949 settlement) and not *for* them.[12]

It was obvious by 1957 that the Dutch were in a far better
position to aid New Guinean development financially and
technologically than the Indonesians were. From a standpoint
of material self-interest, the Dutch should have been eager to
rid themselves of West New Guinea, but they were just as
emotional about the matter as the Indonesians. The latter
were about to attempt an armed invasion when the Netherlands government, under heavy U.N. and U.S. pressure, decided that it would rather yield than fight. One possible
explanation for the Indonesian government's insistence on
taking over West New Guinea is that the campaign helped to
divert popular attention from its failure to deliver on its
domestic promises. The demand for national territory fostered
a spirit of national unity which seemed to make economic
deprivation easier to bear.

Moreover, the rebellion in 1958 in Sumatra and Celebes

---

[12] Cf. Arend Lijphart, *The Trauma of Decolonization: The Dutch and New
Guinea*, New Haven, Conn., Yale University Press, 1966.

against the Djakarta regime caused a rapid expansion of the armed forces, which soon were able to suppress the insurrection. Once the troops were put on a war footing, it seemed reasonable to use them for other purposes—such as the invasion of New Guinea. The invasion was prepared but became unnecessary when the Dutch reluctantly yielded.

Long before then, the Indonesian government decided to take its revenge for the Dutch stubbornness in holding on to West New Guinea. It seized in 1958-60 almost all Dutch property—large and small estates of sugar, rubber, tea, coffee, tobacco, etc.; industrial, mining, shipping concerns; wholesale and retail establishments; banks; export and import businesses; and public utilities. Then it expelled all Dutch citizens and permitted them to take along little more than what they could carry. Their houses, equipment, and cars were left behind to serve new occupants, at least as long as they were usable without adequate maintenance.

This development satisfied many long-held ambitions. As mentioned earlier (page 83), dissatisfaction had developed among friends and supporters of the regime when they realized that independence did not mean that they could immediately move into the front offices of the business concerns and take over the houses, automobiles, and other possessions of the Dutch owners, managers, and technicians. Only the limited number who were given big government jobs had been able to do so. Thus many Indonesians who had waited impatiently for independence were happiest when action against the Dutch in 1958-60 at last enabled them to realize their aspirations. Government leaders, of course, failed to consider the consequences of replacing experienced executive personnel with deserving political supporters, Army officers, and others who lacked the required knowledge and skill.

It has been charged, with much justification, that during colonial days the Dutch failed to train Indonesians for higher technical, managerial, and administrative responsibilities. The depth of local resentment and the call for reprisals in 1957-58 are therefore quite understandable. However, wholesale expulsion of the Dutch, when adequate local replacement was unavailable, amounted to economic suicide. The material loss to Dutch citizens was huge, but with the exception of a small minority, Indonesians suffered even more as a consequence of this 1957-58 action.

Indonesia expanded its educational system sharply during the postwar period, and the reduction of illiteracy is one of the most remarkable accomplishments of the new regime. More than 17 million students are now enrolled in school at all levels, but even after 17 years of independence the number of persons who are properly trained in technical and managerial fields is sorely inadequate for the country's needs.

In 1955 Indonesians went to the polls, for the first and last time, to elect a Constituent Assembly. After years of fruitless arguments, President Sukarno dissolved the assembly by decree on July 5, 1959, abolished the 1950 constitution, and reestablished the constitution which he and his followers had drafted in 1945 at the time of the Japanese surrender and which gave the President dictatorial powers.

In earlier years Sukarno had referred to Indonesia's "Guided Economy" (*Ekonomi Terpimpin*), but in the later 1950's he started describing the governmental system as "Guided Democracy" (*Demokrasi Terpimpin*), a euphemism for one-man rule. This turn of events illustrates a lesson which other countries had already learned from bitter experience: freedom is indivisible. Without economic freedom, political freedom and individual liberty are both very limited and of short duration. If the economy is "guided" from above, political freedom will soon fall by the wayside. In 1960 President Sukarno appointed a "People's Consultative Assembly" to rubber-stamp his decrees. Independent newspapers were suppressed.

Export earnings kept falling. Non-oil exports fell in value from $900 million in 1951 to $775 million in 1955, to an annual average of $562 million in 1959-61, to an average of $434 million in 1962-65. Oil exports fluctuated between $195 and $280 million annually between 1956 and 1965, totalling $210 million in 1965.

The decline in exports had a disastrous impact on the balance of payments. The balance was $99 million positive in 1955, averaged $74 million deficit annually between 1956 and 1960, and averaged a catastrophic $293 million annual deficit between 1961 and 1965. The need to import a large quantity of foodstuffs, the loss of export earnings, and the disappearance of the foreign currency reserve severely restricted capacity to import essential raw materials, spare parts, and machinery. This in turn drove up prices, caused widespread smuggling and black market operations, and diminished the industrial output. Production in many plants was reported down to 20 or 30 percent of rated capacity.

When the five-year plan (1956-60) fell far short of meeting its targets, a much more ambitious eight-year plan (1961-68) was drafted by *Bappenas,* and promulgated. On 5100 pages in 17 volumes the plan conjured a mirage intended to kindle the hopes and arouse the enthusiasm of the Indonesian people. It imposed no belt-tightening, proposed no taxes to finance the planned huge developments, foresaw no foreign private capital investment (the plan's one realistic aspect), but asked for huge government grants and loans from abroad. The emphasis was on consumption and higher living standards for Indonesians—to be paid for by foreign taxpayers.

A team of U.S. experts under Professor D. D. Humphrey of Tufts University conducted a study in 1961 which recommended that sharply expanded U.S. aid to Indonesia be placed on a permanent basis, but by that time the U. S. Congress had become dubious of Indonesian policies, and hesitated. The Soviet Union had entered the picture a few years earlier and provided large quantities of military assistance (which the United States would not supply) in addition to substantial economic aid. This did not cause the U. S. Congress to view larger aid requests with a friendlier eye.

President Sukarno, on the other hand, became increasingly impatient and angry at American stinginess and began to criticize and assail U.S. attitudes and actions. In contrast to other such pronouncements in years past, this did not cause the U. S. Congress to oblige by enlarging aid authorizations; rather, when President Sukarno in a fit of anger told U.S. officials, "Go to Hell with your aid," Congress took him at his word and abruptly terminated all U.S. aid to Indonesia in 1963. Since about 1960, it had become increasingly apparent that Indonesia was turning against the West and entering the communist orbit. When the ending of U.S. aid removed restraints, all fury broke loose in a "Hate America" campaign.

Two years earlier, in his annual Independence Day address on August 17, 1961, President Sukarno had spurred the revolutionary spirit and made it clear that liberal Western democracy and private enterprise were finished in Indonesia. While the country had reached its lowest economic level since 1949, over a period during which one crisis followed another, Sukarno engaged in the most exaggerated hyperbole to make his audience and all Indonesian people forget what his promises at the time of Independence had been. However, some drastic action was needed to divert attention from his failures. His neighbor to the north gave him that opportunity.

Malaya had long been a thorn in Sukarno's side. Its evident prosperity contrasted sharply with Indonesia's growing misery and inevitably invited comparisons and embarrassing questions. Cain could not indefinitely suffer the presence of Abel. When the states of Malaya, Singapore, and northern Borneo joined in 1963 to form Malaysia, Sukarno declared this to be a clear case of *Necolim* (neocolonialism, colonialism, imperialism) and promised to destroy the new country in a "Crush Malaysia" campaign. In the "Confrontation" (*Konfrontasi*), as it was called, Sukarno cut off all trade with Malaysia, including Singapore—which hurt Indonesia at least as much as its adversary. Already by far the strongest military power in the area, Indonesia further enlarged its armed forces with Soviet aid. Military assistance from the U.S.S.R. had been started during the time of the West Irian crisis when huge shipments of arms were supplied and personnel trained by Russian "advisers." Several Indonesian attempts to invade Malaysian territory failed when Britain came to Malaysia's assistance. The campaign accomplished little besides aggravating Indonesia's already desperate economic and financial situation.

British aid to Malaysia brought Indonesian retaliation. The British Embassy in Djakarta was burned by "spontaneous" (i.e., well organized, government-sponsored) mob violence, and most British property was seized. Parallel action ensued against the United States when it failed to support Indonesia against Malaysia. The U. S. Embassy in Djakarta, U.S. consulates in Surabaya and Medan, USIS libraries, and American homes were repeatedly ransacked and looted. American rubber estates and other U.S. firms were taken over.

When the United Nations admitted Malaysia to membership, Sukarno threatened to leave the U. N. and other international agencies, which Indonesia did early in 1965. Relations with the United States, which stood firm in moral support of Malaysia, were heading for a rupture when a *coup d'état* in September 1965 changed the situation in Indonesia decisively.

Despite widespread discontent and suffering, huge unemployment, and deprivation, no organized opposition or resistance to the Sukarno regime developed, at least in Java, nor on the outer islands after the 1958 rebellion had been crushed.

Only the university students, typically critical of governmental policies and better able than other Indonesians to recognize the causes of the economic deterioration, showed open disapproval. Prior to October 1965, most Indonesian experts expected the Sukarno regime to remain in power indefinitely and to continue its policies.

The PKI (*Partai Kommunis Indonesia,* the Indonesian Communist Party) had been gaining strength for some years, particularly since Sukarno's "guided democracy" declaration in 1959, and had won many supporters in the air force, while the army leadership remained strongly anticommunist. On September 30, 1965, the communists arrested and executed six army generals (others escaped) and tried to take over the government. The extent of President Sukarno's involvement in the attempted *putsch* [13] is still unknown; and, in fact, much of the entire action and counteraction remains mysterious and may never be clarified.

Soon after the start of the attempted *coup*—which the Indonesians soon came to call *Gestapu* (from *Gerakan September Tigapuluh,* September 30th Movement)—General Suharto organized a counterforce which succeeded in assuming effective control of the government and the country. In the ensuing few weeks, between 250,000 and 500,000 persons (reports vary: one estimate runs as high as a million) were killed in local action throughout the country.

Many of the victims undoubtedly were communists. Many were Chinese who may or may not have been communists, but were unpopular—as moneylenders, merchants, and members of a hardworking, austere, and economically successful minority usually are. How often the opportunity was seized to settle old scores, to vent personal vengeance or

---

[13] It may be significant that there is no true English equivalent for the terms *coup d'état staatsstreich,* or *Putsch,* so that we have to use the French or German words.

wrath, will never be known. The ferocity of the bloody action surprised most observers and suggests that far more resentment, frustration, and hatred had been built up among the Indonesian people during the Sukarno years than had been believed or was apparent on the surface. A latent anti-Chinese sentiment undoubtedly played a major role in it.

The huge bloodbath settled one thing: there was no way back for the military junta that had taken power, no possibility for a compromise from that point on. The new authorities would either succeed in establishing themselves on a permanent basis or perish in the attempt. No bridge was possible between them and the leftist forces once so close to triumph and now so brutally crushed.

Was the *contre-coup* a spontaneous action in response to the communist *coup*, or was it planned and executed by men who knew in advance of the communists' plans? Did the communists act to prevent a takeover which their opponents were planning? [14] Did the officers act on their own or did they have assistance and advice from abroad? Was the anticommunist *putsch* hatched abroad, waiting for the opportunity that came on September 30? Was the United States involved in this? There are no firm replies to these questions now, only rumors. Whether there ever will be documented answers remains to be seen.

But it seems plausible that the Army officers might not have attempted the counter-*putsch* and would have thrown in their lot with the Gestapu men, had they not received some cooperation or counted on subsequent support from the United States. It is also possible that without some outside aid they might have failed.

[14] *The Economist* commented on October 9, 1965: "There could have been more than a grain of truth in Colonel Untung's claim that he acted to nip a generals' *coup* in the bud." Lt. Col. Untung, a batallion commander in the presidential palace guard, led the military *coup* attempt of September 30, 1965, which was foiled by General Suharto's rapid counteraction.

A communist takeover, whether as a gradual development or by sudden action, had been a distinct possibility for years. Sukarno had formed a close comradeship with Peking, and the outline of a Djakarta-Peking-Hanoi-Pyongyang-Phnompenh axis was clearly emerging. The PKI was Indonesia's largest and most powerful party by mid-1965, and its strength and fortunes were on the rise when the events that followed on September 30 destroyed it. The PKI was dissolved by General Suharto in March 1966.

That there is a connection between the 1965 buildup of U.S. forces in Vietnam and the anticommunist *putsch* in Indonesia appears very likely.[15] The *Far Eastern Economic Review* commented in its *1967 Year Book* (p. 30): "Many observers argued that the complete reversal of the PKI's fortunes in Indonesia could never have been achieved had not the Army and the other noncommunists been encouraged to take decisive action by the American buildup in Vietnam." [16]

Until the spring of 1965 only a small number of American "advisers" were present in Vietnam. At that point many Asian experts—and certainly most of those on the communist side—did not believe that the United States would become involved in Vietnam with major forces. They expected that the United States government, unwilling to commit a large military force to combat, would sooner or later accept the inevitability of a defeat of the South Vietnam government, withdraw, and

[15] Some observers question whether the action should be called an anticommunist *putsch* since President Sukarno remained in office and was only gradually removed from power over the succeeding 18 months. But whatever it is named, the action of the Army officers resulted in the dissolution of Indonesia's communist party.

[16] This may answer, at least in part, questions regarding American policy in Southeast Asia raised by Theodore Draper in *Abuse of Power* (Viking Press, New York, 1967). Draper stated that Indonesia is far more important strategically than Vietnam and that communism suffered its greatest defeat in postwar history in Indonesia. Yet, the United States intervened in Vietnam but did not intervene militarily in Indonesia to prevent a possible communist *coup*.

leave Vietnam and Southeast Asia to its fate, i.e., to the government of the Chinese People's Republic (Red China).

The American armed forces buildup in Vietnam, which began in the spring of 1965, suggested to the anticommunist forces in Indonesia (and elsewhere) that the United States intended to fight at whatever the required cost and with whatever effort was needed. This may have given anticommunists in Indonesia the courage to battle their enemies to defeat. Many other hypotheses have been suggested; some of them sound more convincing than others, but none are provable.

In any case, the political situation in the southeast corner of Asia has changed radically in the past two years. The years 1965-66 could some day prove to have been a watershed for a significant shift of allegiances in Asia and the Pacific area toward the West. Certainly the outcome of the Vietnam issue is likely to have a significant bearing on the future alignment of Indonesia and the entire Southeast Asia-Pacific area.

Prior to October 1965, Indonesia, the largest and best-armed nation in the region, and one of the most populous on earth, was close to Peking and Moscow and seemed about to turn communist in name and fact. Some of the surrounding countries were uncertain or insecure. Today we have there a bastion *against* communism. Indeed, Indonesia, Malaysia, and the Philippines may yet form the *Maphilindo* group which, with Thailand and other countries, could become a Southeast Asia common market—to be enlarged later to include much of Asia—and a bulwark against Red Chinese expansion. The crucial question is, of course, whether an anticommunist regime in Indonesia will be able to stay in office. Having come to power by a *coup d'état* the Suharto government must within a reasonable time win the allegiance of the broad mass of the Indonesian people or yield to others who can. It cannot maintain itself indefinitely by force of arms. The real question is not simply whether the regime can win popular support, but whether it can maintain such support while establishing policies necessary to put Indonesia on the road to economic recovery.

The Indonesian people have been subjected to communist-inspired anticapitalist, anti-Western indoctrination for so many years that they will view with suspicion the reintroduction of private enterprise, free markets, and Western capital, managers, and technicians, particularly since results, in terms of improved living standards, will be a long time in coming. Many Indonesians may have to give up jobs which they have been able to hold until now only because no one competent to fill them has been available. They will lose perquisites they have come to view as rightfully theirs.

There is a tendency in Indonesia—and occasionally also abroad—to view the economic debacle of the 1950's and early 1960's only as a personal failure of the Sukarno regime and not also as a consequence of its aims and policies. It is undoubtedly true that irrational actions such as the several military adventures, emotional outbursts and spiteful actions, the expulsion of the Dutch professional class, and, in general, the government's inability to carry out its proudly announced plans bear much responsibility for the rapid downward slide. But the depth of the failure in every sector of the economy suggests that the methods chosen to achieve the goals were faulty.

It appears that even if far greater competence had been available, the plans to raise Indonesia's economy to higher levels and to provide prosperity for its inhabitants through nationalization of the large and medium-sized enterprises and centralization of command could not have succeeded. Poor execution only made matters worse.

This certainly does not prove that Indonesia would have achieved prosperity had it gone the free enterprise route. However, if analogies with Indonesia's past and with other countries suggest something, it is that the people of Indonesia would today be better off if they had avoided a break with the economic policies that had brought good results to them in the past and have lifted many other countries to higher levels of well-being since the end of World War II. This is not yet sufficiently recognized in Indonesia, and until it is, threatening clouds will continue to hover over its political and economic horizon.

FROM RUIN TO . . . ?

Sukarno's fall from power came as a surprise to most Asia experts. Such knowledgeable observers as Arnold C. Brackman [17] expected as late as mid-1965 that the regime would survive and continue to "guide" Indonesia indefinitely. Few were as perspicacious as American University's Willard A. Hanna, who predicted as early as 1961 "the collapse within a very few years, perhaps even within months, of the disastrous Bung Karno regime" and "the emergence of some new leaders not now closely associated with Bung Karno's failures." [18]

As the man who had led the fight for independence for many years, had triumphed and gone on to become Indonesia's George Washington, Sukarno still commanded much prestige, affection, and loyalty in several parts of Java, even after years of mismanagement and after the *putsch* and counter-*putsch* of 1965. Though student groups and others demanded his immediate recall, impeachment, or exile, the new powers deemed it the better part of wisdom to diminish Sukarno's authority gradually and not to remove him from office

[17] *Southeast Asia's Second Front* (New York, Praeger, 1966).

[18] *Bung Karno's Indonesia*, revised edition (Washington, D.C., American University Field Staff, 1961), p. xiv (proc.). Sukarno liked to refer to himself as *Bung Karno* (Comrade Karno).

until almost one and a half years after the *coup*. Only in February 1967 did General Suharto assume the title of Acting President, though he and his two chief associates, Adam Malik and the Sultan Hamengko Buwono IX, had governed as a triumvirate, with the help of the army, since October 1965.

The change in political allegiance, alignment, and atmosphere is evident and pervasive. Indonesia moved out of the communist orbit and toward friendly relations with the West, called off its "Crush Malaysia" campaign, re-established neighborly and trade relations with Malaysia and Singapore, rejoined the United Nations and other international organizations and, on the whole, tried to regain the confidence of other nations by showing that the time of irrationalism and adventures, of extravagance and flamboyance was over.

No clear picture of the new government's economic policies emerged soon. In fact, the new regime had no policies to begin with beyond official recognition of the urgency of action to effect a speedy economic recovery. The Suharto regime, having come to power by a military *coup d'état,* has always regarded itself as only a temporary bridge to a stable and more permanent future government. Its economic views are not ideologically conditioned but appear to be pragmatic: it seems willing to accept the laws of economics and act accordingly, unlike its predecessors, who preferred to ignore or fight them. Official statements in April 1966 paid tribute to the *Pantjasila's* goal of establishing "a socialistic and welfare community," and at the same time announced that "the government will abandon its attitude regarding medium and large-scale enterprises as if they were its enemies" and praised the operation of free markets unhampered by government control. The test will come when specific measures are adopted which are necessary but politically unpalatable. It is one thing to *talk* about decontrol, a balanced budget, an end to inflation, and a policy of austerity and retrenchment. It is another to carry out such programs against powerful interests.

Indonesia is fortunate in that its economy is still largely rural and that the agricultural sector was not as severely hit by the political upheavals and nonsensical, spur-of-the-moment decrees which created chaos in industry and trade. The farmers went on planting essential food crops and their harvests have been showing a steady—if inadequate—rate of growth.

To summarize: the country's crucial problems are the widening discrepancy between the growth rates in the food supply and in the population, the disorganization and de-capitalization of its estate operations, the run-down condition or disappearance of the plantations that used to produce most of its export crops, the disrepair, diminished capacity, incompetence, and corruption in its industrial, mine, trade, and financial sectors, and the huge budgetary deficits which are largely, though not wholly, responsible for the runaway inflation. The big balance of payments deficits of recent years are the result of export capacity, unwise pricing policies, attempts to impose artificial exchange rates, and the importation of unnecessary goods which served only prestige and conspicuous consumption purposes. The deficits restrained importation of essential spare parts, raw materials, and machinery; this restraint in turn had a dampening effect on domestic production.

At the core of it all is the almost complete disappearance of the entrepreneurial, managerial, technical, and professional class that developed Indonesia's natural resources, manned its major productive activities outside subsistence agriculture prior to World War II, and until ten years ago was still holding the fort against heavy handicaps. While the government's and the new nation's emotional need and impatience to replace the foreigners in their midst soon after achieving independence is humanly understandable, the premature timing and abruptness of the action will continue to exact a high price and to inflict deprivation on Indonesia's people for decades, and probably generations to come.

The command posts in the economy and the managerial and technical positions in industry, commerce, and on plantations were filled largely by officers of the armed forces and others with inadequate qualifications for such responsibilities. Some of them were replaced—particularly after the September 30 *coup*—but as a rule with men of no greater competence.

Corruption is as widespread as ever and virtually universal; the new regime has been unable to restrain it. Soldiers and government clerks are paid between $1 and $5 a month, high officers and officials in charge of large plants or departments, between $5 and $10. Small wonder that they must depend on graft to support themselves and their families. This is the result of runaway inflation, with which salaries were unable to keep pace, and of Sukarno's principle that it is preferable to employ 100 persons at half pay than 50 at adequate wages.

Whether substantial boosts in government salaries would eliminate or significantly reduce the corruption now so long and firmly established, is doubtful. Salary increases certainly would increase demand and pressure to get and stay on the public payroll and would make any program to cut governmental employment more difficult to carry out.

Although a few controls were relaxed, no decisive changes in economic policy were made soon after the *coup* because no advance plans had been prepared, and time was required to devise appropriate measures. The economy did not improve in 1966; in fact, it turned worse in some respects. The banknote printing press kept operating at top speed and inflation accelerated. Prices multiplied almost ten times within a year and the industrial production record was spotty.

It is obvious that the Suharto regime is on trial. Having

come to power by a military *coup*, it commanded little organized support among the broad masses to begin with. To gain time it will probably postpone the elections, originally scheduled for 1968, until at least 1970. In the long run, the new government will need to earn the confidence of the Indonesian people, which it cannot do without an adequate performance in the economic area. If the regime proves unable to lift production and income to higher levels, if misery continues unabated, dissatisfaction will multiply and the strength of the communists, diminished in October 1965, will grow again, possibly to a point where they can stage a successful revolution.

The possible choices for the Suharto regime are limited. To try and bring back the former Dutch owners and managers *en masse* is politically unthinkable, even if it were physically and financially feasible. The expulsion of over 200,000 people in 1958-60, though it proved even more ruinous to the country than to the persons directly affected, is one of those acts which, once carried out, cannot be undone or reversed.

The crucial problems of inefficiency, incompetence, and waste—of low production at high cost—in most of the enterprises which the government seized from the mid-1950's on, cannot be solved without better managers and technicians than are presently available. But most of the Dutch professional men and their families have long since settled in Holland or elsewhere and would not want to chance returning to Indonesia. Some have been coming back since about 1964 and the flow could be increased by appropriate action, but the number of returnees is likely to remain limited. A friendly attitude on the part of the Indonesian government toward the employment of foreign technical and professional personnel, where adequate skills are locally not available, would be helpful. But to welcome and install Western managers would be to invite grave political peril for the regime.

A long colonial past and 20 years of intense anti-European, anti-capitalist propaganda have left a deeply rooted xenophobic sentiment among a population to which action that seems to reek of neocolonialism or leaves itself open to such charge has become anathema. Irrational as the feeling may be in view of the country's needs, it will be hard to overcome. So it seems that Indonesia, having once taken precipitous action, will henceforth have to depend for recovery largely on the talents and energy of its own people, for better or for worse, with only a small icing of foreign technical aid.

Some of the nationalized property should be returned to its former owners. In fact, many foreign companies other than Dutch (American, British, etc.) which were not expropriated but merely placed under Indonesian control are now being turned back. But a wholesale return of all or most formerly foreign-owned property, whether business or personal, is as much out of the question as is the restoration of Dutch colonial administrators to their former posts.

Nor are Dutch or other foreign investors and entrepreneurs likely to move in in large numbers, even if all doors were opened. Some, to be sure, have been showing interest in recent years in participating again in the development of Indonesia's latent resources, particularly minerals and plantation crops. They could make a major contribution to the country's recovery and should by all means be encouraged, for if their ventures prove successful, they could become forerunners of broad-scale cooperation and a bright future.

But nobody can say with any certainty at this time that even if all obstacles were removed, attractive incentives offered, free reign given to private enterprise, and government-held establishments turned over to private hands, that private interests, foreign or domestic, would within a reasonable time take advantage of the opportunities to such an extent that the country would soon rise to prosperity. The political uncertainties and perils in the world, in Southeast Asia, and in Indonesia are too great to hope within the next few years for a rush of private capital to establish in Indonesia the type of economy that has generated rapid growth and ever-rising living standards in Malaysia, Thailand, Taiwan, Japan, and many other countries since the end of World War II. Confidence can be—and in the case of Indonesia was—lost within a short time. To regain it will take many years and perhaps generations. Nor are indigenous private capital and entrepreneurial spirit available in adequate quantities or likely to arise soon. The group that showed the greatest promise, the Chinese, has long been discriminated against, and the new regime has alienated them even more. This should be corrected, but expectations cannot be raised very high.

It appears, therefore, that the government will need to play an important role in the development of the country's economy for some years to come. *But that role should be envisioned as declining, not as increasing.* Indonesia is unlikely to reach the level of prosperity and well-being to which its natural resources and population entitle it unless opportunities, denied in the postwar period, are again opened to private enterprise on plantations, in industry, mining, trade, finance, and shipping. In view of the competition for capital as well as entrepreneurial and technical talent from many other countries, it will take strong incentives, encouragement, and firm guarantees by the government—and the conviction on the part of those invited that the government intends to and *will be able* to live up to them—to start a movement *into* Indonesia that will reverse the flight of capital and talent of the past quarter century.

For many years Sukarno promised the people that prosperity was just around the corner and they believed him. Eventually they became disillusioned. They must now recognize that recovery will be hard and cumbrous and take decades, even if the government pursues the wisest of economic policies. It would be futile to expect recovery unless an ever-growing participation by private enterprise is invited and facilitated.

The Suharto regime inherited a desperate situation which almost defies solution. Indonesia has been living beyond its means for so long and has consumed so much of its substance —in addition to foreign grants and loans—that the obstacles to effective action are staggering. Among the gravest problems is the foreign currency situation brought on by persistent balance of payments deficits which totaled almost $1.5 billion cumulative from 1961 to 1965. This is an enormous amount for a country whose national income does not exceed $5 billion a year. Such a degree of economic imbalance cannot be long sustained.

Export earnings were officially estimated at $485 million in 1966, and may be at the same level in 1967. Service on the $2.5 billion foreign debt,[19] over half of it owed to Iron Curtain countries, called for payments totalling $530 million in 1966 and $629 million in 1967. But the cost of importing essential foodstuffs, spare parts, raw materials, etc., was placed at $590 million a year by the Indonesian government. This leaves a foreign exchange gap of between $600 and $700 million annually. No immediate and significant rise in export earnings, 90% of which come from petroleum, rubber, tin, tobacco, palm oil, coffee, tea, and copra, can be expected. To stop the importation of food, raw materials, and spare parts would mean starvation and bring much of the country's productive machinery to a grinding halt. This seems to leave only one way out: to ask for a moratorium on foreign debt service and for additional grants and loans.

One-half of the $1.5 billion payments deficit in the years

---

[19] This figure is for loans, but does not include claims for expropriation of foreign property or the Netherlands Indies debt which Indonesia had assumed but later renounced.

1961 to 1965 was covered by grants and loans, the other half by using up all remaining reserves, by piling up short-term liabilities, and eventually, by not paying due bills. In 1965 the Bank of Indonesia was no longer able to meet its foreign commitments and the country was, for all practical purposes, bankrupt.

There were no more reserves left to cover deficits and new loans were hard to come by. Some emergency action was needed to prevent utter chaos. When the Indonesian government asked for a rescheduling of its debts, the Japanese government invited the major creditor nations to a discussion, which was held in Tokyo in September 1966. The group has been called the "Tokyo Club" ever since. The first meeting was followed by a second in Paris in December, and by a third in Amsterdam. The U.S.S.R., Indonesia's biggest creditor with claims totaling $1 billion, and other Eastern bloc countries, were invited but did not attend.

The Indonesian government asked for a deferral of its debt service and for new loans totaling $350 million in 1967. Cognizant of Indonesia's bankrupt condition, the creditor nations knew they had no chance of getting their due payments on time or within the next few years. Rather than let defaults pile up, they agreed to a moratorium of principal and interest payments and the rescheduling of debt service to the years 1971-79. Whether obligations can be and will be met on the new dates remains to be seen.

Studies were undertaken by the IBRD (World Bank) and the IMF (International Monetary Fund) in the late summer of 1966 to ascertain Indonesia's immediate foreign exchange needs and to evaluate its prospects. The IMF estimated the minimum first-year needs at $150 million, and the Indonesian government was able to obtain slightly more than that in 1966. The Tokyo Club nations agreed to grant new credits, totalling about $200 million in 1967, of which the United

States would contribute one-third. After an interruption of four years, U.S. aid was resumed with the granting of a $10 million loan by AID (U. S. Agency for International Development) to buy spare parts and raw materials. Previously, 50,000 tons of rice and 75,000 bales of cotton had been advanced on a *loan basis* under Public Law 480 (agricultural surplus disposal).

Two weeks before the Tokyo meeting, Indonesia's Deputy Prime Minister for Finance and Economic Affairs, Sultan Hamengko Buwono, journeyed to the Hague to settle claims for the nationalization of Dutch property. The Dutch had by then—more than eight years after the expropriation—absorbed their losses and were willing to settle for little more than a token recognition. They scaled their claims down from $1.1 billion to $166 million. (Hfl 4 billion to Hfl 600 million), payable over a 30-year period beginning in 1973 and ending in 2002. They granted Indonesia $18 million (Hfl 66 million) in immediate new aid, with more in the offing for later. Indonesia also announced that the former owners of some of the property seized by the government would be permitted to buy it back. It remains to be seen whether many will take up that offer to buy property which probably has deteriorated in the intervening period and compensation claims for which have just been settled at 15 cents on the dollar, payable in installments until the year 2002. But the announcement indicated that at least the years of recrimination and hostility between Indonesia and the Netherlands were over and that both parties were willing to cooperate in Indonesia's recovery.

The statement which Sultan Hamengko Buwono submitted at the Tokyo meeting in September 1966 indicated more clearly than any earlier pronouncements the plans of the Suharto regime. It declared that "a new order has emerged with a pragmatic rather than a doctrinaire approach in solving our nation's problems," and presented a broad outline of the policies the government intended to pursue:

"a) By rendering a more proper role to market forces, create a wider and equal opportunity for participation in the development of our economy by all creative efforts, state and private, domestic and foreign alike.

b) The achievement of a balanced State Budget.

c) The pursuance of a rigid yet well-directed credit policy by the banking system.

d) Establishment of a proper link between the domestic and the international economy through a realistic exchange rate, and thus creating stimuli to reverse the downward trend of the balance of payments."

The government would formulate and carry out an economic stabilization program, to be preceded by an immediate rescue program, with priority given to the control of inflation. "Thus after years of economic neglect the country, its people, and its government now resolve to turn the tide."

Existing distortions in the economy were blamed on governmental planning. To correct them required a reversal of policies by permitting "a more normal operation of market forces."

"My government," the Sultan said, "is determined to take the necessary measures to achieve such a decontrol of the economy." [20] He promised tax increases and expenditure cuts in an attempt to balance the budget. Development outlays would be reduced and state enterprises would set their prices so as to provide a net revenue rather than require subsidies. "Managerial skills to achieve the efficiency which my government hopes for, may still be lacking. The solution will have

[20] Export and currency regulations were in fact slightly eased but price controls, multiple exchange rates, and price subsidies were maintained. On the whole, the politically tough decisions were deferred.

to be found in managerial assistance from abroad whenever necessary and in decentralization of management to facilitate more effective control."

Such statements were designed to make a favorable impression on the representatives of nations with a strong free enterprise and free market tradition and on financial circles. But the proposals still contained no detailed plan of how the government intended to cope with the country's two basic deficiencies:

a) Imbalance between production and consumption.

   The country neither produces enough goods to fill its own needs nor produces and exports enough to earn the foreign exchange it requires. The country consumes too much of what it cannot, and for a long time will not be able to, produce.

b) Imbalance in the government budget, with resulting inflation.

   The government has for many years been spending far more than it takes in, has covered the deficits by printing new money and thus caused runaway inflation with resulting distortions throughout the economy. Income and outgo are so far out of line—the ratio in 1966 was more than 1:3—that redress will be extremely difficult. No realistic blueprint has yet been published.

A discussion of these two major deficiencies follows.

1) *Imbalance Between Production and Consumption*

Sustained economic growth is possible only when a country's production exceeds its consumption. Unless part of the output is set aside for investment and capital formation, and unless goods are produced of a quality and at a price which foreign markets will buy in sufficient quantity to equal at least the cost of necessary imports plus debt service and other obligations, no progress will occur. A country may for some time consume more than it produces by borrowing from abroad and by living on its substance (decapitalization). However, this process cannot continue indefinitely and, unless reversed, must lead to ruin.

These rules are about as basic and almost as trite as Mr. Micawber's doctrine. Still, during the postwar period these rules were honored largely in the breach by Indonesia and many other "developing" countries going through a revolution of rising expectations. As a result those countries were not and are not developing. For example, it makes no economic sense whatsoever for a country like Indonesia to import basic foodstuffs such as rice. It ought to be a food exporter. Since not enough fertilizers, pesticides, vaccines, and machinery are now locally produced, and cannot be imported in adequate quantities for want of foreign exchange (a vicious circle), more intensive cultivation, possibly on the Japanese pattern (horticulture), must be an essential part of a program to bring food supplies and population into a better balance.

Although the situation has some Malthusian aspects that need to be considered, the potential improvement on the supply side should not be underrated. The extension service is poorly informed and ineffective in teaching farmers to grow more productive crops and use modern methods. It is typical that in many parts of Java the cutting knife is still used rather than the sickle, the hoe rather than the plow. Experts have estimated that acre yield of most crops could be made to rise two to four times.

The seizure of the plantations had a detrimental impact on the production of export crops, the greater part of which are now grown by small farmers—inefficiently. If private estate operation were encouraged and made attractive again, and if some of the methods were applied that have enabled Malaysia to expand its harvests and markets in such crops, great progress could be made. To be sure, a rejuvenation of the rubber acreage by replanting with high-yield varieties and adoption of improved tapping methods (high and low tapping) will, at best, take many years to show tangible results—years of hard work and further belt-tightening. But this is a price that Indonesia's people may have to pay for having condoned and supported the perverse policies of the past two decades.

Mineral exploitation could be dramatically expanded by energetic action. Especially suitable for more rapid development are the petroleum reserves in Sumatra and its offshore locations, which are the richest for thousands of miles around. Indonesia could become the Iran or Arabia of the Far East and Pacific region. Among oil prospectors and large international companies there is great interest to operate in Indonesia. Quite a few have visited Indonesia in recent years or investigated its potential. If the government were willing to create the necessary conditions—and if political stability is maintained—the output of petroleum and its products could be multiplied within a few years.

Indonesia, like other less developed countries, drew ambitious multi-year plans to expand its manufacturing sector faster than the rest of its economy. Rapid industrialization was and is still viewed by many as the best hope of prosperity without the painful and lengthy process of adjustment which the Western countries underwent during their industrial revolution. The time involved can be shortened, as some countries have demonstrated, but the painful process of sacrificing consumption while multiplying productive efforts is unavoidable —though the thought itself is alien to many nations outside the Western and Chinese-Japanese cultures. It is not in keeping with the mentality that has prevailed in postwar Indonesia.

Despite the rapid industrial growth which the five- and eight-year plans envisioned, the share of manufacturing in the Indonesian economy shrank from 13.3% in 1958 to 11.9%

in 1965. It is an ironic comment on the change from a colonial to an independent regime and on the promise of centralized planning that employment in manufacturing was reported lower in the 1961 census than in the (preceding) 1930 census, not only as a percentage of the work force but in absolute numbers.[21] The decline may be attributed in part to the expropriation of foreign enterprises and the expulsion of their managers and staffs.

The expropriation cannot be rescinded, as explained earlier, but genuine attempts should be made to make industrial operations again attractive to entrepreneurs and technicians. The word "profit," denounced and despised in Indonesia for many years, must be made respectable again. Even so, to reestablish private enterprise will be a drawn-out process, because the business community, international and domestic, once burned, will be slow to regain confidence and take the risk.

To open the doors will not be easy politically. Army officers who now occupy many of the managerial and technical positions, however incompetently in many cases, are enjoying the spoils of office and will not readily give them up. Nor can a government that came to power by a military *coup* and maintains itself through the Army, afford to antagonize those whose support it needs.

Sentiment against and repression of the Chinese population have intensified in the past two years. Yet this is the local group which can most effectively aid and lead in a development of business activities—as it has in neighboring Malaysia. To ease restrictions, reopen opportunities, and smooth the path for Indonesia's Chinese people will not be popular

---

[21] The total work force meanwhile increased by 66 percent, however. G. W. Jones, "The Growth and Changing Structure of the Indonesian Labour Force, 1930-1981," *Bulletin of Indonesian Economic Studies,* Department of Economics, Research School of Pacific Studies, Australian National University, Canberra, June 1966, p. 52.

among certain powerful groups. But Indonesia now has insufficient talent of its own to ignore the Chinese or to drive them to emigration. To use and act according to slogans may yield some political mileage, but it can be an expensive proposition.

The country's economic fortunes will of course be affected by public policies in many other areas. But the crucial question may well be whether the government in the future will, as it indicated it would, rely mainly on the market forces, or whether it will try to meet difficulties, minor and major emergencies, by piecemeal intervention and by continued or renewed, centralized control.

The adoption of the foreign investment law, in January 1967, indicates that Indonesia's new government recognizes the importance of attracting private capital from abroad. The law promises freedom of management, grants temporary tax relief through exemption and deferral, permits transfer of profits and repatriation of capital, and gives assurances against nationalization. It does require the employment of Indonesians when the needed skills are available, and it mandates education and training of local citizens to replace foreign employees within a reasonable time. A number of foreign companies have since come back, such as Goodyear, U. S. Rubber, Union Carbide, Unilever, Bata Shoe, and British American Tobacco. Freeport Sulfur signed a contract to explore-exploit copper deposits, U. S. Steel is seeking rights for mining nickel, Union Carbide for tungsten. Caltex is expanding its petroleum operations, several oil companies have obtained drilling concessions in the waters north of Java, and Continental Oil Company has secured concessions in Kalimantan. Alcoa is exploring possibilities, as are a number of Dutch and Japanese firms. The State Tin Mining Enterprise, which now controls all tin mining, is seeking private capital to restore the industry to its former role in the world tin market, possibly on a production-sharing contract basis.[22]

David Crane reported in *Far Eastern Economic Review* for May 4, 1967, that "The recent signing of an investment guarantee agreement with the United States—which enables the Agency for International Development to insure qualified U.S. investors against political risks, including government confiscation, war damage, and problems of currency convertibility—attracted within a week *applications totaling more than $100 million* from prospective investors. The majority of the applications related to mining and oil prospects." Mr. Crane described the prospects succinctly: "That Indonesia possesses a great potential for mineral development is undoubted, but the future of the mining industry will depend upon how the new regime is prepared to treat foreign investment, and on the building up of confidence in its sincerity."

2) *Imbalance in the Government Budget*

Budgetary deficits do not bear the entire responsibility for Indonesia's runaway inflation and soaring prices of the 1950's and 1960's. Credit expansion, losses of government enterprises, and greater velocity of circulation contributed their share. But deficits certainly fed more fuel to the inflationary fires than all other factors combined.

Between December 1961 and December 1965 the money supply multiplied 40 times, the budgetary deficit 60 times, prices 100 times. Those trends even accelerated in 1966 but showed an encouraging slowdown late in 1966 and in the early part of 1967.

There have been ample declarations of the Indonesian government, both before and after the *coup* of 1965, assailing the

---

[22] In 1941 the Dutch had mined 53,372 tons of tin; in 1966 only 12,536 tons were mined, despite some improvements in recovery methods.

havoc wrought by inflation and promising to end it. President Sukarno issued an order in September 1965 to stop inflation within one year. But inflation is not as susceptible to oratory as are human audiences.

The *rupiah* was replaced in December 1965 by a *new rupiah* at a ratio of 1:1000. This eased record keeping but accomplished little else. There is no chance of ending inflation as long as government keeps the banknote press operating at high speed.

There is no substitute for a balanced budget. The International Monetary Fund experts who visited Indonesia in the summer of 1966 insisted that the government prepare a balanced budget for 1967. This was done and the estimate showed:

	1966	1967
	billions of new rupiahs	
Receipts	8.0	78.9
Expenditures	25.4	78.9

That a 1:3 ratio between income and outgo can be converted into a 1:1 ratio within one year is very unlikely. Even the experts who prepared the budget—under orders to have it balanced—doubted that it could be done. As submitted to Parliament in November 1966 and adopted, the budget balanced at 81.3 billion rupiahs. Even though a sizeable deficit is the likely outcome in 1967, any approach toward balance constitutes a major improvement over the recent past.

At a rate of 100 new rupiahs to the dollar, the 1967 budget equals $813 million, which is not a large amount in a country of more than 100 million people. It equals only 1.5% of the national product. However, the budget is quite unrealistic: expenditures are likely to be much larger, revenues smaller than shown.

More than one-third of the estimated receipts—$286 million—is expected to come from foreign credits which may or may not materialize. Service on foreign debt (mostly short term) is shown at $119 million on the outgo side.

Revenue receipts from taxes, charges, etc. appear at $480 million to be overstated, particularly in the case of corporate taxes and export duties.

That government personnel expenditures can be kept to $147 million (not counting rice allowances) is improbable. There are an estimated 1.2 million civilian employees on the public payroll, not counting government enterprises, and 522,000 men in the armed forces. The numbers are far larger than they need be, and some cutbacks have been taking place and will probably continue. But to dismiss several hundred thousand public employees when unemployment is already extremely high (estimated by some at 12 million) and few other opportunities are available is politically unfeasible. Nor can hundreds of thousands of soldiers be discharged without creating the danger of marauding bands, uprisings, or revolution. Salaries, doubled in January 1967, are still too low to represent even close to a living wage. Whom can the government depend on if it alienates and demoralizes its civilian employees and soldiers?

Still, there is no chance of balancing the budget and arresting inflation unless the government payroll is sharply cut. But, just as a frozen person should not be brought immediately into a hot room, the public payroll may have to be deflated gradually. Attrition, unfortunately, is small because there are so few other opportunities available.

Unnecessarily high employment in governmental enterprises accounts for some of the big deficits met from subsidies in the budget. Elimination of subsidies will force the firing of more employees and will, in some cases, result in a shutdown of entire plants. Because of the government takeover of most enterprises in the 1950's and early 1960's, there are not many jobs left in private employment.

There is no way that redundant public employees can be used on "other projects" without the investment of large sums in such projects. Resettlement on the outer islands also is an expensive process. Army units can be—and some are being—used for civil works such as road building and repair (better communications are urgently needed). But this activity results in no saving on the payroll while it adds to outlays for tools, machinery, and materials.

The Development Budget for 1967 is shown at $60 million, a paltry amount in a country the size of Indonesia whose productive plant—machinery, trucks and cars, tools, etc.—are in a state of appalling disrepair. Nor can the country realistically expect an influx of large private investment funds in the near future, as mentioned earlier.

I am citing these facts to demonstrate that the situation is truly grave, that there are no easy—or immediately effective —solutions, and that the possibilities open to the Suharto government are limited by factors over which it has little or no control. Some of the measures which appear to be indicated from a budgetary or economics viewpoint, could lead to political unrest or upheaval, and to the end of peaceful government in Indonesia. It will take a great deal of patience and the investment of sizeable funds by foreign nations to help Indonesia on the road to recovery. Only if governments and international organizations provide such funds and thereby make a recovery at least possible, will private investors gain sufficient confidence in the maintenance of peaceful rule in Indonesia to risk their money on large ventures.

Is it worth the money of taxpayers in the Western countries to allow Indonesia grants and large loans which may never be

repaid? What are the alternatives? Without large-scale aid—
and sounder policies—Indonesia is likely to sink into chaos
and sooner or later revert to the forces of violent revolution
rather than advance through peaceful economic progress.

To be sure, there is no guarantee that even sizeable aid
amounts and sensible government policies can prevent a disastrous outcome. But without aid and internal reforms such
outcome is more than likely. With aid there is at least a chance
that it can be prevented *if aid is not used as a substitute for
essential but unpopular reforms.*

A great deal could be said for "letting Indonesia stew in its
own juice," as an example to other nations of the results of
such policies as the Indonesian government followed after
gaining independence. A country's citizens are responsible
for their government and must assume—and suffer—the consequences of whatever actions it takes. Ignorance or misguid-
ance by beguiling demagogues are no adequate defense. In
cold judgment then the punishment may appear not entirely
undeserved.

But guilt is not the basis on which international questions
of such magnitude and consequence can be or should be decided. The real issue is whether the self-interest of the Western nations and the peace of the world would be so adversely
affected by a fall of Indonesia into chaos and a reversion to
the communist orbit, that even large investments at high risks
in the next few years are defensible. The eventual cost of an
alternative course could be far greater.

The suffering of the people of Indonesia could well serve
as a warning to other countries which may be tempted to pursue similar policies. The history of Indonesian economic policies in the past 20 years gives a good demonstration of the
consequences of the course Indonesia set for itself in the years
following its independence.

Select Bibliography

A good general survey of Indonesia and Malaysia is provided by two volumes prepared under the auspices of the Foreign Areas Studies Division, The American University, Washington, D.C.: *U.S. Army Area Handbook for Indonesia,* 1964, and *Area Handbook for Malaysia and Singapore,* July 1965 (Washington, D.C.: U. S. Government Printing Office). Each volume contains a bibliography.

Most statistical data in this book were obtained from *Statistical Yearbook 1966* (United Nations, 1967), and from publications of the United Nations Economic Commission for Asia and the Far East (ECAFE), Bangkok. An annual report of this commission, *Economic Survey of Asia and the Far East,* is indispensable for a study of the economics of the region, as is the *Economic Yearbook* (Hongkong: Far Eastern Economic Review).

ECAFE also publishes a quarterly journal, *Economic Bulletin for Asia and the Far East,* which contains feature articles and current statistics. In addition, in 1965 ECAFE prepared a volume entitled *Industrial Development in Asia and the Far East.*

The most informative news magazine in the field is *Far Eastern Economic Review,* published in Hongkong.

A new journal (since June 1965) which carries important reports and articles is *Bulletin of Indonesian Economic Studies,* published three times a year by the Department of Economics, Research School of Pacific Studies, Australian National University, Canberra.

A study of the *First Malaysia Plan 1966-70* (and its predecessors, the Malaya Plans for 1956-60 and 1961-65) prepared by the Economic Planning Unit in the Prime Minister's Department is essential to an understanding of the Malaysian Government's intentions and policies. Further, much valuable information can be gleaned from the annual reports of the National Bank of Malaysia.

The general literature of the economics and politics of Malaysia and Indonesia in books and journal articles is extensive. A few general works are cited in the text or footnotes of this book. Some recent books are:

Alisjahbana, Takdir. *Indonesia: Cultural and Social Revolution.* Singapore, Oxford University Press, 1966

Crosson, Pierre R. *Economic Growth in Malaysia.* Washington, D.C., National Planning Association, 1966

Grant, Bruce. *Indonesia.* Melbourne University Press, 1964

Higgins, Benjamin H. *Indonesia: Crisis of the Millstones.* Princeton, N. J., Van Nostrand, 1965

Hughes, John. *Indonesian Upheaval.* New York, McKay, 1967

Linder, Willy and Fritz Steck. *Indonesiens Irrwege.* Zurich, Kuchverlag Neue Zuercher Zeitung, 1967

Milne, R. S. *Government and Politics in Malaysia.* Boston, Houghton Mifflin, 1967

Purcell, Victor. *Malaysia.* London, Thames and Hudson, 1965

Vittachi, Tarzie. *The Fall of Sukarno.* New York, Praeger, 1967

Wheelwright, E. L. *Industrialization in Malaysia.* Melbourne University Press, 1965

Williams, Lea A. *The Future of the Overseas Chinese in Southeast Asia.* New York, McGraw-Hill, 1966

Index